The ^little Guide to Finding Our Lost Souls

The *little* Guide to Finding Our Lost Souls

*transformative soulful practices
gleaned from one woman's
mostly ordinary life*

Julie Farray Roick

ISBN: 9781667831626

Editor Laurie Chittenden
Book design Sally Stetson Design
Cover illustration Tara Mirakian

*Deep gratitude for my husband who
gave me the space to come home.*

Table of Contents

Preface

Permission

The true path to progress is paved not with certainty
but doubt, with being open to revision.

Lulu Miller, *Why Fish Don't Exist*

Take a moment and give yourself permission to embark on this adventure to find your lost soul, permission to formulate new practices, new questions, new observations.

We are going deep. Get ready for the ride. Take a breath. Open your heart and mind.

Thomas Moore, a *New York Times* best-selling author of many spiritual books and a former monk, gave me freedom. His book *A Religion of One's Own*, gave me the permission to discover and formulate my own path and practices, to embrace spiritual differences and to allow me to discover my own way. He writes, "To be religious even in a personal way, you have to wake up and find your own portals to wonder and transcendence."

His book, as well as momentous life events, allowed me to break the chains of my religious past which no longer suited me, and, most importantly, to know it was ok. This is an important step for you as well. Not necessarily to break with religion (of course, you may not consider its teachings chains), but to give yourself the permission to approach this journey with kindness and openness. This is your odyssey, no one else's. No one gets to tell you how to proceed. I said, no one, not even your mom.

The Call to Awaken

*A hero is someone who gives his or her life to
something bigger than oneself.*

Joseph Campbell

You are the hero of your own story and everything you have
ever been searching for is within you. What I am talking about
is coming home to your True Self. Capital T. Capital S. The
life Joseph Campbell refers to giving up is your figurative life, the
way you have been living. You too can come home, just like every
hero does in every story. Finding our lost souls starts with giving
ourselves permission to discover our paths; in our way, on our
own timeline, giving us the space to awaken to the call. When
we give ourselves this space, this permission, we give others
permission. This space allows others to also find their souls. This
is a win-win.

I had to stumble, be humbled, become vulnerable and liberated
to an awakening. I have loved and lost people in my life, had
chance and purposeful encounters, just when I needed the lesson.
This is happening to you, too. One such clue is you picked up
this book, which may be your sign or synchronicity or divine
intervention.

Call it what you want. You are here now.

According to *Merriam-Webster's Collegiate Dictionary* to be
enlightened means *freedom from ignorance and misinformation.*
In Buddhism, it means a *final blessed state marked by the absence
of desire or suffering.* While I don't know if we can go there, I do
know we can be freed from ignorance and misinformation and
it is all about waking up. Awareness is the catalyst for changing

your life. And while I think it would be cool to be in a blessed state marked by the absence of desire or suffering, I'm not sure you or I want to live in that space on a daily basis given our real-world lives. So, let's stick with *Merriam-Webster* and let's get to it.

The Importance of Practice

It's what you practice in private that you will be rewarded for in public.

Anthony Robbins

I had a yoga teacher once, I just loved (well, almost in that way), and she taught me a huge lesson. Before her I never understood why they called taking yoga classes "a practice." To me, I thought it must have meant some deep spiritual thing, so I asked her one day. She said, "No, it means you practice the poses knowing it is a never-ending journey. They will never be perfect." Well, sort of a deep spiritual thing but in the context, not really. You could use this term *practice* for just about anything in life, any creative venture, a new habit you want to acquire, or a physical challenge. I have applied this concept to my spiritual journey as I would encourage you to do the same.

The knowledge that practice won't ever be perfect gives space for your practice to become purposeful, transcending the goal of perfection and embracing the journey. Practice is just that, practice, and it results in growth. To truly awaken, we have to set up a practice and practice purposefully.

For a long while, I knew I was on a spiritual journey but never really felt as though I was in the groove of it all because of a lack of commitment to the practice. I started a practice, stopped. Read another book, tried its teachings, practiced, stopped. Start. Stop. Start. Stop. Maybe this is typical, maybe not so much for religious folks. Having been raised in Catholic and parochial schools and a quasi-religious home, as I grew older I questioned all of those religious rules. I threw out the religious playbook and was left on my own to discover my awakening, my own religion. A helping hand would have been pretty sweet then. I'm here to be your helping hand.

You will want to invest in a journal you are excited to work with. Because my career is schedule-based and I'm old school, I purchase a blank dot journal so I can write my schedule the way I want to look *and* add the important action lists, gratitude notes, phone calls, etc. to my journal. My dot journal gives me freedom to create something that works for me. When I finally started taking this spiritual thing seriously, I set up "dailies" in my work schedule notebook to remind me to be mindful of the things I wanted to work on, some of which were ridding bad habits (stop saying the F word) to more spiritual (meditate, give love and space). It's important at this point in your journey to set up a practice, a practice that works for you NOW. Your practices will change, as life does. Finding our lost souls takes a daily commitment with the flexibility for change when needed. Listen to your gut on this one.

This is what my "dailies" currently look like:

	S	M	T	W	T	F	S
write	✓	✓	✓	✓			
read	✓	✓	✓	✓			
work-out		✓	✓	✓			
♡	✓	✓	✓	✓			
?	✓	✓	✓	✓			
★	✓	✓	✓	✓			
↑smarts				✓			
paint	✓						

Working on giving love (heart), asking questions (?) and creating space (star), are becoming more routine. Getting smarter and practicing my watercolor painting, not so much, but this keeps me accountable to my goals, both spiritually and personally. This isn't a one and done kind of thing. This journey takes practice and while I share my example of a habit tracker, you ultimately need to choose and more importantly, implement your own version. Give yourself some time and space to decide what to include. Finding what works for you doesn't need to happen overnight.

Additionally, throughout the book, there are questions for you to ponder to aid in finding your lost soul. These are opportunities to pull out your journal. Of course, you can answer them all, some or none. This is *your* journey, so it something resonates within, explore whatever that is a bit deeper. While I don't believe in getting too caught up in the past, rehashing mistakes, or worse, clinging to the victim role (defining yourself by your past or anything else you can't control including your immediate family or unfortunate events), I do believe in reflection and learning from our past mistakes. I'm hopeful the questions throughout this little guide will help you start reflecting on what is important to you and how they may influence you soulfully.

Now, let's continue the adventure we are all on.

NOTE: *Throughout this guide, I tell personal stories to illustrate the pathway to our transformative soulful practices. I have changed the names of the innocent and the not-so-innocent.*

Awaken to the Observer

Missing the Signs
How did I get here?

Talking Heads

There is a man on his rooftop waiting for God to save him from the rising flood waters at his feet.

A life vest floats by him. He dismisses it, "God will save me."

An empty kayak passes him, he pushes it aside, saying "God will save me."

The rescue squad in a helicopter hovers over him, extending the life-saving ladder, rescuer shouting, "Buddy, grab the ladder!"

"No, God will save me," the man screams back.

When the water overtakes him, and he arrives at the pearly gates, God asks, "Why are you here?"

The man says, "I was waiting for you to save me!"

God told him, "I tried. I sent you the life vest, the kayak and the rescue squad."

Our lives are filled with such signs we can't see because of the veil over our lives; the misconceptions, preconceptions, stories we have been told, inherited and never challenged belief systems. This veil distorts reality, your reality and mine. We are going to learn to lift this veil. Hopefully, you are a faster learner than I am.

It's 1986, I'm living in Southern California, graduating in a semester from the University of California, Irvine and getting married within a month of graduation. I'm drooling on my pillow, more so than the usual, and rubbing the sleep from my eyes with

the back side of my hand, when I quickly realize I can't feel my hand against my face. 'That's strange' I think. I try again, still no feeling. Fish hooking one side of my mouth with my pointer finger to force a smile, I realize the gravity of the situation - I can't move the left side of my face. I run to the bathroom only to discover half my face is paralyzed! Terrified, I knew immediately I had to get to the emergency room. I was living (in Catholic sin) with my fiancé and we were getting married in seven months, so in my mind, this was a crisis. I did not want to look like a freak at my wedding. I said to my fiancé, "Can you take me to the ER, something is really wrong."

He said, "Really? The waves are great right now."

The waves were beckoning him, and Surfer wanted to surf. So he went surfing and I went to the emergency room, alone. It's ok. I don't need his support.

My initial attraction to Surfer was he seemed nice. He also seemed pretty broken and often times broke, which didn't matter to me. You know, a fixer-upper. Every time we went on a date, he told me another story about his troubled past, run-ins with the law or other missteps, bad luck or bad calculations. Raised with a dozen years of parochial schooling, this Cafeteria Catholic was a rule-follower, so this was a departure for me, slightly intriguing, indulging my inner rebel if there even was one to be indulged. After all, the cafeteria part really just involved Catholic Guilt, with Christmas and Easter sprinkled in for fun.

I like a project. What woman doesn't like a project? Plus, we will grow together, right? And he is nice after all, way nicer than the first boyfriend. But I was 16 then, 21 was way different. I really knew what I wanted. I wanted a nice project.

I spent hours alone, chilled from the nerves or maybe just because they keep the emergency room unusually cold. Frightened and tearful, a parade of doctors came in to check out the anomaly. What could possibly be wrong with what appeared to be an otherwise healthy 21-year-old? I was moved from room to room, as more urgent matters needing more urgent attention took my place in line, a little facial paralysis needed to wait. It didn't appear to be going anywhere anytime soon. My emergency wasn't really their emergency.

Five hours later, a neurologist finally figured out what was wrong with me. I was diagnosed with Bell's Palsy, a virus in the main facial nerve causing paralysis. The prognosis was vague – could be forever, could be a month.

"Miss, have you been under any stress?"

Uh, yeah, I'm getting married to not-the-man-of-my-dreams in 7 months, a month after my college graduation. No stress here. I got home, Surfer asked how the ER visit went. The waves were great by the way. He felt sorry for me, but he wasn't great at showing comfort, and at the moment, I wasn't great at seeing this as a moment of reckoning. I was now more stressed than ever. The idea of half my face drooping, unknowingly slightly drooling out of one side of my mouth at any given time, getting married in this condition compounded my stress. Not to mention the fact, I was questioning what the hell I was doing getting married. Oh yeah, I can't disappoint anyone.

I called my parents in Northern California, Mom and Dad to the rescue. They had a tight group of friends who quickly recommended acupuncture. I'm sure there was even some banter as to why I was suddenly inflicted with this.

"She is stressed out."

"Can you believe her fiancé went surfing instead of taking her to the emergency room?"

"We think she is making a mistake but would never tell her that."

"Doesn't she see the signs?"

A visit with Acupuncturist in a nearby town was quickly arranged. I walked in, not having a clue what to expect. The office was humble, dank, and quite sparse - a small indoor plant near the desk, curtains dividing the treatment tables, a shelving system lined with bottles of varying sizes, all labeled with Chinese characters. The office smelled herbal-ly. Acupuncturist took one look at me and said, "I will have you smiling in thirty days."

Relieved, I would be taken care, I half-smiled back at him. Please tell me I am not drooling.

A week into my acupuncture treatment on a visit home during Thanksgiving, I ran into a high school acquaintance at the mall. More stress. But this stress was one with some societal pecking order. You see, I've never had a lot of friends, nor was I ever really popular. The ones who understood me were few and far between. I was never the head cheerleader, nor the class president or even close, even though I did try to be both, thinking I was more than I was, but no one else thinking the same of me. I've never been super cool, pretty, or even that funny. Little and cute maybe, but none of the other adjectives.

This acquaintance, who I'd run into, happened to be one of the cool ones, sweet but still cool. Upon seeing me and my face, she looked horrified but didn't ask. She clearly pitied me, wondering what was wrong. So now, not popular, not cool enough and slightly scary looking – a geeked out trifecta! I didn't dare get into the details of what was going on. I just wanted to pretend nothing had actually happened. I certainly didn't want to answer the backstory question "What is stressing you?" Admitting I was making a mistake wasn't something I was going to do with myself, let alone an acquaintance.

Gratefully, by Christmas, as promised, Acupuncturist did have me smiling again. My signature feature was back. Well, at least in theory anyway.

There were obvious relationship signs I was ignoring (remember the bad luck, run-ins with the law etc.) but why did I ignore the biggest red flag yet - going to the ER alone? I was so angry and disappointed with Surfer, but I didn't say anything. Women get angry and disappointed with their partners, right? How angry? How disappointed? Break-up disappointed? What are the deal breakers? How many do you need to have before you say enough is enough? I didn't want to mess up my marriage plans. The money already spent; guest list solidified. Plus, it wasn't like he was abusive or anything close to that. He was a nice guy. No, I don't want to mess that up. And certainly, I DO NOT want to disappoint my parents.

I am confident there have been times in your life when you too have asked "How did I get here?". The signs were all there, from the Universe or whomever, whispers or sometimes even screams, wake-up calls if you will, the signs showing you are lost. Looking back, I recognize several but at the time, I didn't want to admit seeing the signs. In hindsight, you too may be able to recognize your signs. We all know when we are receiving one, it's almost screaming *WARNING WRONG WAY*, but we are not ready to see the signs, hear the signs, or certainly not admit the signs. We can usually feel these warnings, usually in the gut but we still deny them. Admitting it makes things difficult or just maybe more difficult. Yet, this is just another story we tell ourselves.

Identifying the Influenced Self

Ego is the false sense of self, based on mental concepts.
Eckhart Tolle, *A New Earth*

The reason we don't want to see the signs or can't is because the veil of our Influenced Self is blocking our view. Who is your Influenced Self? Your Influenced Self is Ego. It took many years for me to truly understand this concept and the role ego plays in a spiritual awakening. In fact, when I first picked up Eckhart's book in 2005, I had no clue what he was talking about. Now I do (I told you I was a slow learner). And I'm here to help you understand this concept, too.

When we are born, we are pure, unencumbered, our soulful True Self. We haven't encountered the influences yet that start to shape our belief systems and thoughts. The veil, our Influenced Self, is the overlay that has been placed on top of our True Self, overlay from years and years of experiences, observations, judgments.

To lift the veil, we will need to awaken from our Influenced Selves and become The Observers.

I am using the term Influenced Self because this term embodies what has happened to your True Self, given time, relationships, and experiences. Your Influenced Self is defined by the stories we attach to our labels, the stories based on how we see ourselves, our experiences, and our interpretations of these experiences.

As we grow, our True Self gets lost and replaced by the Influenced Self. We begin to formulate how we fit into the world, how we relate to others. The Influenced Self is the person we put out into the world, the hat we wear at any given time and the stories we have projected on to those roles. Take a moment and give some thought to the roles you play: Child, Spouse/Partner, Parent, Employee, Friend. What experiences have molded your perception of these roles? What is expected of you? What have you been taught about them?

Here is the tiniest of samples (feel free to play along and add your own):

Hat	Story
Child	I don't want to disappoint my parents. I must ___ for them I can never please them.
Spouse/Partner	Their needs come before mine I am so lucky. They are so lucky They drive me crazy.
Parent	My children are my life's work They define me. My children belong to me.
Employee	My career means everything My value is my paycheck. My work is important I am important to the company.
Friend/Community Member	I am reliable They need me.

These all get compounded when we layer on our familial stories and experiences with others. Suffice it to say, we all live wrapped up in our Influenced Self projections, with different roles or labels and the myths that go along with them. We put these on daily and put them out into the world. Recognizing the Influenced Self is our first step. Once recognized, our first goal is giving these stories less power in our day-to-day life.

We all have different personalities, innate characteristics that make you uniquely You. The Influenced Self is the Self with the stories attached to those characteristics. For example, *introvert* is a personality trait. An introvert isn't necessarily shy but more quiet, introspective, thoughtful. Shy is a story people tell about introverts. If you are an introvert and your parents always said you were shy, your Influenced Self is going to have a story about being shy, even living up to those expectations, integrating shy into your personality which may have never come to fruition had you not been told you were shy. Imagine being born into a different family. What would *introvert* mean to them? That's the problem with stories (and some parents), they aren't necessarily correct, and our True Self becomes lost in our Influenced Self, our story. I'm not playing the blame game here. But I do want you to start thinking about some of the assumptions you have made about yourself, or others have about you and begin to question them.

Recognizing the Influenced Self in Your Younger Self

You can't put an old head on young shoulders.

Gaelic Proverb (told to me by a friend)

Oh, how different life would have been had my older self been able to hop into that DMC DeLorean à la *Back to the Future* and showed up on my younger self's doorstep.

Hey, Julie, I'm your Future Self and you need to learn some lessons, quickly.

Let's stick to the facts of your life:

You have a dance major.

You got Bell's Palsy seven months before your wedding. You are a daughter, sister, cousin, friend and fiancé.

These are facts. But you included your stories with them and that is why it will take you so long to awaken.

All of those stories you tell yourself aren't true. You know the ones about you and your future husband, your community, your parents. They are stories you make up in your mind. They could also be stories someone else may have told you. No matter the source of fabrication, they are fiction.

There are three sides to every story - yours, theirs, and the truth.

The stories in your head are based on perspective, that of your Influenced Self. Other people's stories are influenced by their perspective, their Influenced Self. And the truth, well that is somewhere in the middle. You may never know the truth. That is ok. You just need to know neither side is completely true.

My older self then hops back into the car and back to the future. My younger self most likely stunned, would not have known what to do with that information. Besides thinking they know it all, most youngsters don't yet have the practice or perspective to process like adults and haven't had the worldly experiences necessary. I obviously didn't. An exception to the rule may be those old souls. Maybe those are the ones who get the EZ Pass to awakening. Given my situation, I was here to learn some lessons and seemingly fumbled for coins to give to the attendant *every single time* a lesson was presented. Maybe you feel the same way.

It is true, I was diagnosed with Bell's Palsy seven months before I was getting married. At the time, I made up stories to excuse Surfer's behavior and to continue planning that fateful walk down the aisle. A sign? Of course, it was a blazing scarlet flag! But I wanted a family of my own and worried this wouldn't happen any time soon if I didn't walk down that aisle. Truth? No. This was a myth, a story I had told myself to validate my actions. I was 21! Who knew what could have happened in the next 20 years? I also didn't want to disappoint my parents: all the wedding money, the plans, the invitations, the living in sin, etc. Of course, the deposits made, the venues set, the invite list done are facts but disappointing my parents was my perspective. These were stories, ones I had fabricated with no factual knowledge of how my parents would have reacted. I kept these stories to myself. And that is where we get into trouble. Unsubstantiated stories and thoughts cause stress. Can you see your Influenced Self in your younger self? What would your Older Self say to your Younger Self? (be nice)

This is a great exercise in recognizing the falsehoods which your younger self was living within, including the stories you made up, and helps you recognize your Influenced Self. I often say to myself *"who was that person?"* Now, I have a clue.

We are in good company because everyone does this. Yes, everyone. Even monks do this, but ok, maybe not Jesus or the Buddha. The labels and stories we make up in our minds are based on our human experiences, labels like: Child, Sibling, Cousin, Spouse, Parent, Friend, Insert Job Title Here. Yes, these are true human labels, human roles. These are hats any one of us must wear on a daily basis. However, our myths include stories we tell ourselves, turning fact into fiction, fiction into drama. How do you know when a story is false?

Whenever you tell yourself a story, and the story conjures up any type of stress or anxiety, your Influenced Self is in play, holding an attachment to a falsehood.

Separate fact from fiction and you will awaken. What differentiates your human experience from your spiritual experience is the acknowledgment of the stories that go along with these Influenced Selves.

My 30 plus-year-older-self can now identify fact vs. fiction, truth from drama. Even though I've been through this awakening, scratch that, continue to awaken, I have to be reminded on a daily basis to step back and identify the drama.

As humans, we all think we need these myths to survive in this world. We think we need our Influenced Self and the Influenced Selves of others. Of course, we do need to wear those daily hats, those roles we play, but we don't need the stories we have attached to those roles. On your spiritual path to unveil your True Self, identifying, observing and awakening to the Influenced Self is the first step.

One clue to help you identify Influenced Self is if you feel:

offended,

inferior,

superior,

attachment,

jealousy,

envy,

stress, anxiety, guilt or worry,

your Influenced Self has put you in this state, and you and only you, can control your response.

This is our first practice to finding our lost souls, identifying you from You, unconscious from Conscious, Influenced Self from Observer.

Waking up or lifting the veil, needn't take a lifetime, especially now that you are becoming aware. We have all been sleeping through our lives, telling ourselves stories and now, with awareness, we can stop. It's never too late to start this process.

It was going to take me quite a while to wake up to this new reality. There were plenty more signs, lessons, slaps in the face, sent by the Universe to help me, but with a heavy overlay of my Influenced Self things weren't quite that clear.

So, Dancer ends up marrying Surfer despite the enormous sign of going alone to the emergency room. With a degree in Dance, I taught for some time but had to dabble in banking and bookkeeping

to help pay the bills. Within a few years, Dancer became Mama and Surfer became Suit and we were in love, I with my children and he with his work. We were living parallel lives.

By year twelve (I told you I was a slow learner), Mama was really lost. Raising four children in East Coast Fancy Pants Town now, where trying to keep up with the Joneses wasn't my gig. Moving there had been Suit's dream and to do all of the keeping up. I felt like I didn't belong and struggled to find purpose. Finding purpose in my children, I am defined by my children, were stories I told myself. They weren't true, but I didn't know this at the time. The truth was I couldn't remember who I was, or who I ever wanted to be.

I had few friends and struggled to relate to most women there. We didn't have the fanciest house, it was a fixer-upper with plans to fix it up never coming to fruition, but we wanted a good school system for the kids, so it worked for us. With my parents across the country in California, my father reminded me many times how I broke my mother's heart when I moved away, first to Southern California but now to East Coast Fancy Pants Town.

It was time for payback. It was her turn to break my heart. "Jule, you better get out here, she isn't going to make it through the weekend," it was my Dad, calling from Las Vegas. I was panicked. It was Thanksgiving weekend and I needed to get a flight from JFK to Las Vegas, the worst weekend to travel. I said, "O.K. Daddy. Is she able to speak to me?"

"No, honey" his voice cracking, "she is on life support."

"I will get there just as soon as possible," I said, "I love you."

We hung up and I started bawling.

They were in Las Vegas, spending a fun weekend together,

knowing those weekends were limited. She had battled bone cancer for just under a year and gave up the fight, refusing any more medications or therapies. I had spoken with her the night before he called, saying good-bye with the usual "I love you" and "have fun." I was happy she was able to be in her favorite city, New York, albeit Las Vegas-style, seeing all the over-blown shows and gambling with my Dad, one of their absolute favorite past-times. My Mom had a stroke in their room while he was out, the guilt of not being with her at the time, haunted him until his death over 20 years later.

Guilt haunted him before her death too, as he had cheated on her when I was just a baby, and she took him back. I didn't find out about the affair until I was much older, and my mother was gone. Judging my father only lasted moments though. He was always a good father to me.

She had me as a last-ditch effort to save the marriage. Her effort worked but I can't really take the credit. The credit belongs to my Mom, she worked hard to keep the marriage together. She always said, "Marriage is a lot of work." She was right but it took the knowledge of my Dad's indiscretion for me to understand the depth of why she thought this. I knew why I thought so.

So, Youngest went with me. I knew Suit couldn't handle all the kids for a week. We crammed into a shuttle bound for JFK and then crammed into the only seat available on the plane. She was crying, hot and uncomfortable. I was anxious, and in deep emotional pain, already feeling the void of my soon-to-be missing relationship. The man next to us was huge and his mass was spilling over into my seat. I was trying to make Youngest comfortable to settle in for the long flight without bumping into him when I just could not keep it together any longer and started crying. She took one look at me, closed her eyes, and fell asleep in my arms.

We made it to Las Vegas on time, well at least to see her on life support. I was in disbelief. Yes, I knew she was sick. I knew she was going to die but I didn't really know it, at least I didn't want to believe this was happening to me. I didn't have the right words at the time and just sobbed at her bedside, as they took her off life support, unable to comfort, unable to be comforted. That evening, my brother and I walked around Las Vegas pushing Youngest in a stroller through Paris then on to the Bellagio fountains, completely surreal. My father crying himself to sleep in the room we shared, the last one he shared with her, in total disbelief the world was continuing without her. We were all in disbelief.

How was I to continue without her? She was my rock, my mentor, and yes even at times my friend. We talked every single day. I know when I moved away to Fancy Pants Town, I broke her heart, but she never held me back from doing what was right for my marriage. How would I navigate this married-with-lots-of-children thing without her?

She was gone, and my Cafeteria Catholic-ness was not holding me up, or able to pull me through the grief. Maybe it was because of my Dad's affair, she insisted I go to Catholic schools, for a moral compass. Her inherited belief system was based on guilt and in typical matriarchal form, she passed her belief system on to me. She wasn't super religious. She was superstitious. Old-school Catholic guilt was woven into her messaging. "You really should go to church, Jule" (even though she only went on Easter and Christmas), and her infamous "Shame on you" when she didn't approve of something I had done. The idea of Hell terrified her and not believing in God, or "His" rules was a ticket straight to eternal fire.

I didn't buy into her religion, the patriarchal rules, unsubstantiated beliefs, the hypocrisy, but I went along with it for her. When I moved in with Surfer, the guilt-ometer sky-rocketed. I remedied this faux pas by marrying in a Catholic church and for extra heavenly points, baptizing all of my children. I missed her terribly and felt orphaned and alone, surrounded by my children and the menagerie of pets Suit would bring home to fill his compulsions and my plate. How could I stay married without my Jiminy Cricket? I had no playbook. No faith.

I searched for completeness in spiritual books, hoping for a newfound faith. Kept a gratitude journal. Meditated. Practiced yoga. But Suit kept me busy with his obsessiveness and children defined Mama. These stories I told myself allowed little time to find a semblance of a newer, happier Dancer.

I decided I needed a change. A big one, but I was unsure of what was next. The spiritual exploration would take a back seat for now. I didn't have time for spirituality, to find my God. God would have to find me.

Without God or my mother, I started plotting my shift. Suit and I planned a family vacation to Quaint Town during school's Easter break to check out its livability. My sister and I discovered this beauty of a town on our way to a rowing camp together. Having all the conveniences of a Fancy Pants Town with its boutique stores, great schools, and safety, Quaint Town also offered natural beauty and most importantly, anonymity. It was mud season there and far from beautiful, but Quaint Town lured me anyway.

Strangely, I lost the diamond from my wedding ring at my son's preschool as we were leaving for our road trip. Without a thought, I took the ring off and put it into the car's ashtray, sealing it closed.

I am happily married living in Fancy Pants Town. Another story.

We spent the week in Quaint Town discovering its cuteness, talking to locals, most telling us, "if you think it is beautiful now, just you wait." They were right. I decided to take the easy way out of "marriage is a lot of work" by moving there with my children, thinking Suit would visit on weekends if he was willing to travel.

He supported the fact that I needed a change as I never fit into Fancy Pants Town. My mother would have never approved of a long-distance marriage, never have fit in to her Leave-it-to-Beaver ideals. She was a traditional stay-at-home mother and wife, fully responsible for the children, cooking, cleaning and working for my father for his business part-time at home. Modeled perfectly, I stepped into a similar role with ease and without question at twenty-one. But now at thirty-five, this traditional marriage model wasn't working for me. It was my decision alone whether this idea was good for my marriage. I, Me, My.

I was giddy, anticipating the move. When I chatted about the move with Aussie, a friend with the same casual sensibilities of my California ways, she said, "You better take a good look at your marriage if you are that excited about moving. I think the sun shines out of my husband's ass." Wait, what? Married people think like this? It never occurred to me. "Marriage is a lot of work" was my mantra, was my story. I didn't think the sun shined out of Suit's ass.

My Influenced Self, the stories I played in my mind, kept me from recognizing all of these signs for an exceptionally long time. You would think, wanting to move away, or a friend telling me to look at my marriage would have offered me some clues. The veil was THICK! So was I. But the Universe had a few more tricks up her sleeve.

I was soundly sleeping one night before the move when I felt a tug on my blankets. I gathered them up, pulling them over my shoulder, slightly chilled and quite groggy, more bothered by the inconvenience. Another tug, this time much stronger. I began to come out of my deep slumber, now slightly more annoyed, jockeying for my share of the blankets. I then realized something besides Suit was pulling on the blankets. They were being pulled toward my feet. When I finally truly awakened, I was stunned.

The most gorgeous light was hovering over the foot of my bed. The light was twinkling like a star but golden in color, other-worldly, pure and innocent-looking, an indescribable beauty of brightness, like the deepest glow of a beeswax candle. It was little, too, like something maybe a fairy would leave behind in her haste to fly away. I sat there in wonder, contemplating who or what could this be? I was mesmerized and for those moments I thought, Why me? Who are you? What is this? And then - swoosh - out the window. I sat there staring at the window, hoping for another glimpse, a surprise curtain-call. Reflecting for some time, I finally fell back asleep comforted in the wonder my mother may have just visited me.

The next morning, I said to Suit, "The weirdest thing happened to me last night. I think my mom visited me but I'm not sure. A beautiful bright light woke me up and then flew out the window."

He said, "Great, you are moving to Quaint Town and leaving me with a ghost in the house."

A typical response, but I wasn't surprised. He was getting stressed about the upheaval this move was causing to his lifestyle. His stories.

Later that week, I went to my usual workout with Gym Crush, my personal trainer (I was living in Fancy Pants Town, after all), and we chatted about the ethereal visit. He had lost his parents in his late teens and twenties, so he could empathize with the feeling of being alone and the longing to see them again, if just for a moment. He often spoke of his father, he clearly missed him.

I asked him, "What do you think it could be? Do you think it was my mom?"

He said, "If it was, don't ever be afraid of how she visits you." I wished for more visits from her if that was the case, wanting to relive that night again and again.

A few days later, I consulted Metaphysical, about the visit. Metaphysical is a friend I would consider way further down the spiritual path. With her long, silver, crooked hair, gorgeous soul-searching eyes, and sans wrinkle complexion (not because of Botox), she seems to be from a different dimension. She is my go-to source for anything spiritual, always calm and contemplative, reflective and wise.

I described the event in vivid detail to her.

I asked, "What do you think it was?"

She said, "Whatever it was, it was trying to wake you up."

I said, "Well it did. It woke me up. I was sound asleep!"

She said, "No, no, no. I mean the light was trying to wake you up". She hesitated, "Let's see, how do I put this? It was meant to wake you up - from the life you are living."

The weight of that statement sat with me for a moment, 'the life you are living.' What could she see that I didn't see? Did she mean being at Suit's beck and call? Or was it caring for a growing menagerie, puppy after puppy, kitten after kitten? Oh wait, she must mean the four children in seven and a half years? So, wait, 'marriage is a lot of work' doesn't mean that much work?

It was that kind of wake-up call. Whoa.

You would have thought this wake-up call would have been enough to put me on track. It wasn't. While I felt blessed to have it, I didn't really understand it's deeper meaning despite Metaphysical trying to teach me. She didn't come out and explicitly say, "You have a huge veil over your life, and you need to lift it in order to be awakened." Waking up really doesn't work like that. You can't tell someone they are sleeping. People must be ready and open to learning. It's true about weight loss, exercise, a new habit, spiritual practices and yes, even miracles. But it was going to take more than this little miracle to wake me up.

Quaint Town moving plans, my mom's death and a tiny miracle all primed me to begin questioning the life I wanted, the life I thought I was supposed to be living. I mean really, when was the last time I did something for me?

I started living for myself. At least that is the story I told myself, still from my Influenced Self but with more emphasis on Self. As in Self-ish which, spoiler-alert, brings even more self- induced stress. I began living from the Influenced Self that substantiates things, the one that emphasizes what *I think I deserve*. The one that is still sleeping.

For over a year, the smell of chlorine welcomed me to the Fancy Pants Town Y, as did Gym Crush. Twice a week, I would spend one hour with him, putting me through the rigorous paces of a killer workout, where I would share everything. It was my escape from the busy-ness of married and Mama life. I looked forward to this time, every time.

It was those two hours I would miss. More specifically, I would miss Gym Crush. I was moving and now making the rounds saying goodbye, my two youngest in tow.

He had never met my children, so he was being his goofiest self. I had seen this side of him before while we trained, at times walking out together passing by a former ornate living room turned daycare center, he would make the children giggle with his antics. Now, with mine, this seemed even more special.

Weeks earlier he had taken me to swim out in the ocean for the first time. He knew I was terrified but was kind and patient with me. My mother was terrified of the water too, actually closing her eyes during her showers, she passed this water hatred on to me. More stories. I asked Aussie to be there, and I introduced them. I don't know why I wanted her there, maybe I wanted her to see what I was talking about, when I did talk about him, which apparently was more often than I thought.

No one knew, not even Aussie, but I had been fantasizing about him. Yes, in that way but in so many other ways. He had the attributes I wished for in a partner. He was fully present, listening with intent and purpose not just to me, but with anyone he encountered, taking time to fully connect with whomever was around.

He was a child-whisperer too, they were absolutely mesmerized by him. He loved children and it was clear when he interacted with them, calling them by name, and showing off his physical comedic skills à la Jim Carrey. He was super funny and always made me laugh. I wasn't used to this wittiness, double meanings, deeper meanings, playing with words. Taking funny to a new level.

When he confessed, "I have my share of demons," this vulnerability made him even more attractive. I wanted to be his heroine, someone he could count on, like I counted on him.

He had a very sexy hero complex. I loved witnessing the way he helped people in the gym, even total strangers. He understood there was more to life than I, Me, My and it was as if I was witnessing this for the first time but every time, we were together. This was foreign territory for me. I was consumed with my children and taking care of Suit's requests, I felt I couldn't get a breath except for those two hours a week where I saw a whole new world. I had him to thank for opening my mind.

I was a bit anxious, as this was 'goodbye' and I was not prepared for it. We hugged, he made the children giggle one more time and we said it... 'goodbye.' Walking out of the Y for the very last time, I wanted to take this moment in. I looked back at him. His thumb and pinky splayed near his face, head tilted, using that universal sign, he mouthed the words "call me."

He did not just do that, did he?

My heart raced.

Could he possibly feel something for me?

But wait, I was married, with FOUR children. Suit and I were planning to build a supposed "dream house" in beautiful Quaint Town. Complicating matters, Gym Crush was also married, and they were trying to start a family. However, appearances are deceiving, as most Fancy Pants Town marriages model. I busied myself with children avoiding Suit's whims. Suit and I lived parallel lives in a transactional marriage. You make the money. I take care of the house and children. Gym Crush's marriage was breaking from the stress of trying too hard. Relationships are forever.

When I did call, Gym Crush said, "I'm not sure what it is, but you can't leave without me seeing you one more time. We need to meet." I said, "I've been thinking about you but couldn't say anything. I didn't think it was right."

"I get it," he said, "but we still need to meet. I have to tell you some things."

I secured the younger children at play dates. Oldest stayed with Metaphysical for the afternoon. I ran some errands, stopped at Starbucks and met him at a secluded park, a park I had driven by a million times but never noticed. Now I noticed and will never forget this life-changing park. I was sick-to-my-stomach nervous.

What the hell are you doing? How cliché - meeting up with your trainer.

He was dressed in khakis; his short-sleeved shirt hugged his biceps. I was in shorts and a tank top, revealing just enough. We lied down on a blanket he brought, too close to each other, teasing one another, not appropriate for a client-trainer relationship, but perfectly appropriate for who we were becoming. I could smell his yumminess, a mix of Old Spice and him.

He confessed he had deep feelings for me and felt a pull he could not describe. I confessed my fantasies. He told me he would travel 3.7 trillion light years to find me. I kissed his soft, wet lips. He said my mouth tasted like baby's breath, like clouds. I felt his kiss down to my toes. We were there for hours, the comings and goings of others not a deterrent, barely even a distraction. We both had no idea where this was going, if this was going, but we crossed the line and there was no turning back. We said our goodbyes knowing deep down they were really hellos.

That afternoon, picking up the children, packing up the car readying it for our trip the next day, I was changed. I felt something I had never felt, like the Universe interjected and I was not the same person. Even if I never saw him again, I was forever changed. It opened my mind to possibilities. Never in a million years would I ever cheat on my husband. Well now I did. What does this say about any of my so-called truths? What else do I tell myself that can be challenged? Where the hell is my moral compass? I have control.

I drove away, a single rowing scull on my car rooftop, four children, three dogs and two cats, to my new home, fantasizing about a new life.

I settled into life in Quaint Town. The children were in Waldorf Schools and during the day I had just enough time to exercise before picking them up. Quaint Town was pretty far from, well, pretty much everything, but I liked it that way. I didn't have to fit in, be cool or pretty enough. I had my children, and they were my life there, and together, we were just enough.

Gym Crush and I started a love affair, over the phone at first and then it morphed into a beautiful, confusing, pulled-together-by-the-universe, the-grass-is-greener type of love affair.

We first agreed to meet about a month after I left Fancy Pants Town, we would meet halfway between. I would get someone to watch the children for the day while I "went shopping" and he feigned a long-distance golf match. Drama, stories, lies.

We met in a parking lot, he parked his car and jumped into mine. He kissed me. I don't think either of us could believe this was happening. I was driving like an old lady, super careful, nervous, not wanting any possibility of an accident to disrupt this moment or day or worse our spouses get a phone call from the police about our untimely death! We found another park to hang out in, new strangers coming and going, before long we just could not take it anymore, so we found a hotel. At least it wasn't a by-the-hour hotel, although that is what it was for us.

I am married. You are married. What are we doing? Because neither one of us drink, we knew exactly what we were doing. We were escaping from our problems into the arms of someone we had grown to love, someone who had listened to us, someone who for an hour twice weekly for over a year, truly got to know. It was liberating, nerve-wracking and completely out of character for both of us, Cafeteria Catholic and always faithful Gym Crush.

Afterward, I showered, he was there holding a towel for me when I got out. He said, "I will always take care of you" as he patted my wet skin, kissing me everywhere. Am I dreaming now? Don't I do all the taking care of?

We stopped for a bite to eat. He sat across the table from me, his dreamy blue eyes watching my every move. So many firsts. What kind of world am I stepping into?

Driving home, I called my sister. She knew. She was the only one who knew about the affair. She had her own problems with her cheating husband she was not leaving any time soon and so she was living vicariously through my story. I was even more ga-ga now. This was a real problem. There was no way I could keep up the charade.

The following weekend while Suit was visiting, he could tell something was wrong, really wrong. I asked for a divorce from him. He was in shock, begging me to reconsider. Of course, he did not see this coming. He didn't know I was miserable. I didn't even know I was miserable. Marriage is a lot of work.

Even though I had asked for the divorce, I hadn't told Suit about my affair, we weren't divorced so technically it was still an affair especially since Gym Crush hadn't jumped out of his. Yes, it was an affair. This would be a fact.

Of course, an affair isn't the right thing to do, no one thinks an affair is the right thing. Justified maybe, but not right. Affairs fill the gaping holes in marriages. Ours had holes, maybe more than most, maybe not. Gym Crush's holes included deep-seeded thoughts never to be admitted, hairline emotional fractures morphing into a full-blown break, never to be restored. A lack of trust. Integrity. My marriage's holes included an already fragile bond replaced by love for my children, above anyone or anything, the physical and metaphorical Pillow Mountain of stacked pillows between us at night, representing so many other things between us.

But still, yeah, justified. At least that is what we tell ourselves. I am right and you are wrong.

For me, it was knowing that if I feel this way about someone else, I just can't stay in the marriage, there was no going back. I had experienced a shift in consciousness, realizing the possibilities of a different life even if we didn't end up together. I would rather be alone than be with Suit. And that is it, the bottom line. After all, I didn't end my marriage for Gym Crush, I ended it for me. I wasn't leaving Suit for Gym Crush because I didn't actually know if that would work. That must be the criteria. Not if the grass is greener, not if the lover leaves the wife. No, I would be happier alone.

And then 9/11 happened.

Everyone was grieving, and I was holed up in Quaint Town, raising four children and completely distracted with the fantasy of what could be.

I got a call from Suit his voice upset, telling me what was happening in The City. Luckily, he no longer worked there but the devastation still deeply affected him as it did the whole country. At least his children were safe, and he had hoped we could work things out even though I was explicit about my done-ness, he erroneously still had hope. And then the shit hit the proverbial fan.

Gym Crush's wife found out about the affair. A few guesses and she discovered with whom. His wife called Suit. I'm in control.

Suffice it to say, the next few months weren't pretty. Suit made all kinds of threats. He was devastated but I really can't tell you if it was from the loss of the marriage or the loss of his routine. Justified.

Gym Crush was terribly conflicted. He had a clientele he had built. His sisters and their spouses were holding him accountable to them and they loved his wife. He was struggling with all of it, the escape from his reality with me and the integrity and pledge of faithfulness he had taken with his wife.

Months later in Fancy Pants Town, both separated now, Gym Crush was house sitting and I was visiting. Both of our spouses knew now but the relationship still felt sneaky and not as fun as when they didn't. I know, pretty gross. His wife showed up one day and started screaming at him and crying, I think I even heard her slap his face. He was trying to maintain control and she seemingly was banging on his chest. I was cowering in a bedroom. What the hell am I doing here? How did I get here? Who have I become?

When he came back to the room, it was so clear what we had done, what we had been doing, for the very first time. I felt sick. Not really knowing her made it easier, I guess, but hearing her, a real person, experiencing real pain, made it real to me. Our escapism, our inability to recognize the problems in our marriages, our justifications as to why we get to do this, has real consequences. Relationships aren't forever. I, Me, My. Well, what about the others?

I left. He followed. I tried to escape to a friend's house. He found me. We talked for a while, and then left together to talk some more, but we both knew this was the end. It had to be. The fantasy had collided with reality, and it felt really shitty.

It wasn't what either of us wanted, but it was necessary. The stresses were too much, and we both needed to figure out what we really wanted and how best to go forward with whatever that might be. We needed to get our acts together. For me, getting my act together meant continuing to work through a divorce. For him, well, that meant trying to fix his relationship if he could. We broke it off before Christmas so he could try.

Throughout Christmas, I did not hear a word from Gym Crush. He was trying to do the right thing. It was a terrible time to be alone. But I made this bed. I was reeling from all my losses. My mother's passing. A move. A divorce. The end of an affair. I was struggling to get my feet under me, navigating what single motherhood looks like. The whole country was reeling from 9/11. It was New Year's 2002, and I was watching Larry King interview a slew of self-help

gurus, Tony Robbins, Deepak Chopra and Andrew Weil, to help
pull the country through this tragic time. Selfishly, I tuned in for a
pity-party remedy. And then Tony Robbins said it, the sentence that
changed my trajectory,

"I think the very first thing you have to do is take control of your
body first, because when you take control of your body, the mind
and the emotions respond."

I returned to the gym.

The gym is the reason my life changed. Yes, my mother died.
Yes, I had an affair. But really and truly, training with Gym Crush
gave me physical strength but also confidence and security to
tackle anything. Returning to the gym gave me a dose of what I
really needed then – strength. To this day, as a personal trainer
for over 18 years, I see this happen all the time. Women come to
me to get stronger, and it impacts every single part of their lives.
Right now, I needed to be stronger in every way.

Reflecting on the end of the affair gave me a glimpse into many
firsts. This was the first time I understood what it meant to give
space to someone. Yes, physical space, but it was emotional space
too. This space was about letting go. Whatever brought us together
in the first place was either going to bring us back together or
would simply be a lesson learned. Who knew?

It was also the first time, I realized how my actions affect the
other. At the time, I didn't feel this way about Suit or really even
my children. My children were my world, and I was by far the
main caregiver. I knew they would still see their father, but I

wasn't concerned they would miss his parental skills. I felt I could do this parenting thing alone. Another story? Maybe. At the time, I figured Suit would have a similar role apart from them as he had with them. Again feeling justified.

This justification stopped however when it came to Gym Crush's wife. I felt the gravity of the affair the night she confronted him and how what we do affects others, deeply. *What we do matters.* My actions matter in my immediate family and reverberate beyond, to those I don't know. It did not even occur to me, how it might have affected the relationships he had with his sisters, friends, clients. Why I was so insulated and self-absorbed can only be explained by the stories I told myself about my busy-ness with my children, my husband, and the story about how I deserved to be happier. My stories kept me from looking outward to see The Other. It would take years beyond this episode to get my head out of my ass and really realize there is more than *I, Me, My.*

After the affair ended, I threw myself into my children and a quiet, less pretentious life in Quaint Town. At least in Quaint Town, if I don't have what others have, it was not as obvious. Judgments. I still didn't know too many people, by choice. My children were in Waldorf schools, and I had to drive the 45 minutes daily filling most of my daytime hours, spending just enough time at drop off to get to know parents who also commuted to the school. Playdates wouldn't be happening. The children would have to make do with their built-in playdates, their siblings. During the day I did have time for myself, I started exercising consistently. I started reading spiritual books, again. Essentially, I started *really* taking care of myself. I know now that isn't a selfish thing. That is a self-preservation thing and ultimately it is a win-win. Healthier

Mama, Healthier Life.

Looking back on the affair, which I am not encouraging by the way, allowed me to shift away from the way my marriage and children consumed me, to focusing on my needs, even though they were still being viewed through the veil of my Influenced Self. I was clearly still telling myself stories (I told you there was plenty of misinformation and ignorance in my experiences). Stories about being justified, about a force beyond our control. You can judge us for the affair, I'm sure plenty of readers are, but it felt like cosmic influence, or interference, and was yet another sign. Maybe not to be with Gym Crush (spoiler alert: we married in 2006), but to start to come home to myself. To wake up! This would have never happened if my mother was still alive, never. But not because of her rules, because of rules *I thought* she had for me.

All these stories are superficial and our endless thoughts trying to justify events are just more stories, more fiction, more drama and mostly self-induced. And during all these stories, we are sound asleep. Completely oblivious to our deeper more spiritually connected life. You do get to choose - unconscious (Influenced Self) or conscious (Observer). Waking up to the Observer, awakening to the reality of the Influenced Self and really being aware of this, does not mean the Influenced Self just goes away. This is a daily challenge – the daily *observation* of the Influenced Self.

When I started my affair, I justified it by recounting all the reasons I was unhappily married, having never shared my truest feelings with my then husband. I had stories in my mind about *his* stuff and how his stuff was making *me* miserable. These were my stories. This isn't to say these things did not happen (he was obsessed with his work, he was compulsive), but it was my reaction, my Influenced Self's reaction to these problems that exacerbated the myths, creating drama and stress for myself. I didn't yet know how to *observe* and *respond* versus react.

The mantra my mother had given me of "marriage is a lot of work" permeated my every marital move. It took an incredibly long time to realize I was living for the expectations, the stories, *I thought* my mom had of me. These were truly self-imposed expectations, but I was not capable of even seeing these stories. Yes, Thomas Moore's book liberated me from my religious hang-ups, but had my mother still been alive, I would still be sleeping, with all those hang-ups. Her death (and it would take years for me to realize this) liberated me. She had to leave me to free me. I simply was not awake enough, aware enough to recognize this hold on me. This epiphany came years later in an unexpected place, my astrologer's office. (and no, your awakening does not need to include astrology).

I'm sitting with Astrologer listening to all the things I did not know about myself, but she seemed to know. She runs a Jungian Center, and her natal astrological readings incorporate archetypes and mythology. She relays the story of Persephone and Demeter and how it is symbolic to me and my life. Quick recap of this story, Persephone is stolen from her mother, Demeter, by Hades. Persephone is forced to live in the underworld with Hades. As a compromise, Demeter gets to see her daughter half of the year and the other half she goes to the Underworld to become Queen

of the Underworld. As she is telling the story, I'm getting caught up in '"why is she telling me this?", "which one of my daughter's is Persephone?", "why would I agree to let them go, but wait, haven't I already? While I spend over 3 1/2 hours with Astrologer, filled with more stories, archetypes and personality traits, I cannot help but say to her near the end, "I've always thought my mother had passed away to let me live my life. I know that sounds crazy, but if she hadn't died, I would have never left my former husband."

A few days later, still reeling from the fact that someone on this planet knows me way better than me, I wake up from a dream and realize none of my daughters are Persephone. I am Persephone. My mother let me go through death and because of this, I've pursued a life I would not have otherwise. Her passing allowed me to be on my path to become Queen of my world, my deeply introverted Underworld and to discover my True Self. Yes, she loved me, and I loved her, but I NEVER wanted to disappoint her. I always worried I would have let her down if I left my husband. This was not her stuff... this was MY stuff. They say, "hindsight is 20/20." It took 20 years to get 20/20 on a situation where I felt cheated out of having my mom around. But her last gift to me was dying so I could discover myself and live the life I was supposed to live, even if it meant without her.

Discovering a deep truth about your relationship with your mother may be different, I'm pretty sure you aren't sitting in Astrologer's office hearing a similar story. But this story should give you pause to consider the stories *you tell yourself* about your mother (father, guardian, insert-influence's-name-here) and if they are really true. Remember, there is your perspective, their perspective, and the truth. Your True Self is being held captive by these stories, your Influenced Self holds on to believing.

These holds, myths, stories, are all here to trick you into believing your Influenced Self actually matters. Your Influenced Self is a resource we use to help us manage our daily life and relationships. It is a tool to help us navigate this world and give us opportunities to discover our True Self, to learn about one another, but your Influenced Self isn't You. How we use this tool ultimately is within our control, based on our actions. When you start bringing awareness to the signs in your life, the holds, the myths, the stories, then YOU can begin to awaken.

In my role as a daughter, I had made up stories about my mother. These were myths my Influenced Self held on to. This kept me from discovering my True Self. We spend so much time fabricating falsehoods to justify our actions, we lose ourselves, our True Selves, buried in the fakeness of it all.

The reference to my mother's hold is just a metaphor for the hold our Influenced Self has on us. This is a biggie.

The stories we tell ourselves, including guilt about the past or worrying about the future, is the grip of the Influenced Self and prevents us from being present. By being present and becoming The Observer, our True Self has space to show up.

Becoming the Observer
When I let go of what I am, I become what I might be.

Lao Tzu

Take a deep breath. Close your eyes and feel your breath sinking into your body, imagining the air coming into and out of your lungs. Keep breathing, not thinking about anything, anyone, any situation. You aren't wearing any hats, playing any roles, telling any stories. You have no expectations or judgments on you at this moment. Stay with your breath for as long as you like without thinking, telling stories. This space, the place where you are no one or no-thing, is your True Self, your spiritual self, the place where soul resides or God, or your light or a piece of the Universe, or whatever terminology works for you. Take this moment for as long as you like.

This moment of quiet and space gives you a glimpse into your True Self where our thoughts no longer exist, the thoughts that keep us in the container of the Influenced Self. The Influenced Self that believes:

there is a pecking order in our relationships or in our community,
we can control our relationships,
I am right and you are wrong,
the judgments we have about ourselves are truth,
the judgments we have about others are truth,
we are in control,
Blah, blah, blah.

You can always come back to your breath, reconnect with your True Self, your Consciousness, your Higher Self, Soul, God, Energy, Universe. Stop, take a breath, step back from the story, and breathe. There You are. You are awakening to You; you are becoming the Observer. This is your practice, your homework if you are into that. Whatever you need to call it, make it your new habit, come back to your breath and reveal your Soul.

Becoming the Observer gives space to the situation. This could be literally physical space (you walk away for a moment), or emotional space (you give the situation some time without reacting). You simply observe. More space means less drama. Less drama means more peace, more peace means more Truth. More Truth means more love. When *you* change and do the work of your non-reactive and peaceful self, your outside circumstances change, ultimately creating stronger bonds in your relationships. You will notice shifts in the people in your life.

This discovery puts you in the observer's seat. Awakening to it, begins to separate your True Self from your Influenced Self. Your True Self is seen from the lens of the Observer, your consciousness. Take that in for a moment. Awaken to the Observer, the one who holds space for your True Self in the moment without attachment, judgment, or control. You are waking up. You are becoming conscious.

But everyone lives from their Influenced Self, right? Yes, they do. Now that you are aware of this, you will observe it in everyone. This is a good thing for our purposes, since it gives you plenty of practice in awareness (but not for judgment, just observation).

Next time you witness conflict or stress, take a moment and

step back from the situation. You do not need to respond right away. Just give the moment some space and go to your breath. Your True Self will guide you through it.

Why are we given so much practice? It is part of our human experience, part of our spiritual evolution. We must have these situations to learn to rise above it. But you must practice this rising, often. Take heart, you are rising above your Influenced Self to your True Self, your soulful self, where everything in life becomes deeper, more meaningful and more connected.

Can people really change? Yes, everyone can, but only with awareness and practice. Most people stay asleep and in the drama. It isn't our job to enlighten our friends and family to this newfound realization. It's our job to awaken for ourselves and thereby model what this looks like, without judgment. You will learn quite quickly, the more you model this awareness, the more peace you will have in your life. The more often you realize these moments of conflict are fleeting you understand all moments are fleeting.

Can I stop the stories I play in my mind about what I think others are expecting of me? Yes, but it starts with a deep awareness of the stories as they unfold. This starts with stepping back and looking only at facts. You will add this to your practice – every single day. Stop. Become aware of the story. Acknowledge it. Don't judge it. Release it.

Does growing out of these come with age, or self-confidence? No, growing out of all of these stories comes from awareness. The stories you tell about your situation are fiction. Mine, of course included my first husband, my societal insecurities, the expectations I thought my parents had of me. The facts are I was married, I am a daughter, sister and cousin and community member. But then things got very gray. Awareness of the roles you play and the stories you tell yourself is the beginning of your true journey. Recognizing how the Influenced Self shows up, all day, every day is the awareness needed to break free from the human experience and to become a human who is being, a human who is conscious.

Through observation of our Influenced Self, we gain control over our actions. As the Observer, we create space for our True Self to show up and we can choose peace over drama.

When we rise beyond the grip of Influenced Self to become the Observer allowing space for our True Self to show up, we can begin the next phase of spiritual development. We move through recognizing The Other beyond *their* Influenced Self, ultimately acknowledging The Other as another soul, struggling with the same Influenced Self societal constraints for whom we can feel compassion and love. We transition through what is typically found in most relationships – attachment, judgment and control, and towards letting go, acceptance and surrender. When we recognize The Other's place in our world beyond their Influenced Self, we can transcend the stories and relate peacefully with one another, as One.

Awaken to the Observer
Practice and Prompts

Take out your journal. This week we will add the following spiritual practices to your "dailies".

1. Recognize the Influenced Self
   (stress, guilt, worry)
2. Go to your breath. ALWAYS, go back to your breath, stay in the moment, and release the stories you are making up.
3. Release the need to be right or to try to solve the moment.
4. Resist the need to know the truth because you may never know it.

For example:

        S   M   T   W   T   F   S

Stressor

Breathe

Release

Truth?

As you awaken, ponder these prompts
to help you identify the Influenced Self.

What roles do you play daily?
What labels do I put on
          myself and others?
What are the stories behind these roles
     and labels? Include any assumptions,
     inferences, or expectations.
Who gave you these stories? Did you
     generate them on your own or were
     they given to you?
What are the obvious falsehoods you
     can recognize?
What is the correlation between your
     thoughts and stories, and your
     actions?
What can you say or do to avoid the
     story associated with this role or label?
How are you identifying with these stories?

Describe the Influenced Self you put
out into the world.

Journal about a situation that upset you.

  Is there a way you could have
    handled this situation differently?
  Did you feel it in your body before
    it was coming on, giving you
    time to change course?
  How could you have handled these
    feelings differently?

  Use the spiritual practices above
to help you with your
Influenced Self emotions.

Influenced Self Values

Our Influenced Self clouds our ability to see clearly, and this is why we miss or ignore the signs. The projections we put out to the world come with a whole host of values we seemingly shoulder without question, complicating the unveiling process. Within the confines of living in our Influenced Self world, we tend to hold on to these values, values taught to us by our family, or community, substantiating the stories about the attached roles. The following is a list of Influenced Self values (it is not exhaustive). See if you can identify where they fit in your world and how they may be limiting your ability to live authentically.

Accountability   Ambition   Career

Challenge   Commitment   Competence

Credibility   Dependability   Determination

Efficiency   Excellence   Initiative

Leadership   Legacy   Loyalty

Order   Perfection   Perseverance

Power   Popularity   Preparedness

Punctuality   Recognition   Reliability

Respect (when expected of others)

Resourcefulness   Risk-taking   Success

Time   Wealth

These aren't bad values. Living in this value set gives you opportunity for growth, which is our human mission - evolution. Our job is to begin recognizing these values, noticing them, without judgment, and how they are coming from our Influenced Selves.

Bring awareness to the two sides of those values: what is in it for me? what is expected of me?

Pick a value and work with it.

What are the stories attached to this value?

We Are One

Recognizing the Other

I see You.

The Na'vi People, *Avatar*

In the movie, *Avatar*, the people have this deeply spiritual greeting, I see *You,* your capital Y-You, your soul. It implies that we have an understanding as soulful beings, that we are in on the secret: we are ultimately one in the same. You don't need to be Na'vi to grasp this concept, of course. When you recognize The Other, the beginning of a life living in Truth is unveiled. No, you are not the center of the Universe, unlike your insular Influenced Self might argue and mine did for far too long.

Once we awaken to the Observer, we begin to recognize the Influenced Self in others. But this isn't time to play the blame game. As you have probably heard before, we are all here as spiritual beings having a human experience. So, it isn't time to start pointing fingers at the people in our lives who haven't quite awakened to the call. How can it be enough for me to wake up to the call and not worry about others doing the same? We can only control what we do. We cannot control anyone else. Working on our awakening is our work alone.

Our loved ones can push our buttons pretty easily because we have so much vested in the relationship. So it is seemingly during the least important of times when we can practice our newfound knowledge with a total stranger. The Universe presents circumstances where we must acknowledge The Other and instead of closing our hearts, we can choose to open them, to spread loving peace. While our close relationships often try us the most, it is both situations, with the ones we love and the total stranger, where we need to take advantage of recognizing our role in these relationships and how we respond to them matters.

Attachment becomes Letting Go

A monk mind practices detachment. We realize that everything – from our houses to our families - is borrowed.
This is detachment, when you observe your own reactions from a distance making decisions with a clear perspective.

Jay Shetty, *Think Like a Monk*

As Jay Shetty suggests, practicing detachment brings us peace. This is exactly what I am talking about with observation and our reactions. I, however, prefer the word non-attachment or letting go. Detachment implies not feeling. This isn't true. You will still feel, but you will get better at not reacting to your feelings. When you come back to your breath, to the presence of the moment, you can still feel, in fact, maybe even more intensely (good or bad) but you can control your response. Our response is the only thing we have control over. Acknowledging that everything is borrowed, gives reverence to those moments and a deeper appreciation of what is.

We have all suffered losses, some self-imposed (a divorce), others more abrupt or painful (the loss of a loved one, sudden or not). We can hold on to what we think was supposed to be, or we can find peace in what really is, the reality of our situation. The need to cling to our attachments brings endless suffering. Relationships change and they also end, we can suffer in the loss of it, or we can choose to let go, turning our pain into peace. One of the biggest areas to practice this is with our children.

In 2008, Oldest moved out to take a gap year, pursuing snowboarding before attending college. That decision alone was a lesson in non-attachment; letting her make her own choices, dealing with the consequences, watching from a distance the repercussions. This was the beginning of the leave-the-nest successions, each one different, each one painful in its own way.

In Khalil Gibran's book The Prophet he writes, "Your children are not your children. They come through you but not from you. They are with you, yet, belong not to you." I'm pretty confident my Mom and Dad did not read Khalil Gibran's The Prophet, but his philosophy seemed to be their philosophy - your children do not belong to you. Years later, in a rare moment, my father lectured me about the mistake I made by making my children the center of my universe, as he blamed that strategy for my failed first marriage. There are way more reasons for that failure than putting my children first, but that was one of them. I had put my children above everything else. I understand now why I did put them first and more importantly, now why I do not. A new "we" are the team (Gym-Crush and I), not me and my children.

My parents let me, and my siblings make our own choices, good, bad, and ugly. They said very little, no matter how deep the parental heartache, a strategy far from today's Lawnmower Parent. (A Lawnmower parent is one that paves the way for their child, so the child experiences no obstacles.) Flying from the nest was an implied must and fly we did, some further than others, never once being told not to. They let us learn, no matter the fall. We also knew we could count on them to help us with the pieces. They knew our lives were our lives, apart from them but not separated from them. That being said I still had, Jiminy Cricket aka Mom, on my shoulder for most of my decisions as I had not awakened to my Influenced Self (I know, shocking, right?).

Gym Crush and I, navigated raising now five children, juggling a business and learning to accept whatever role Suit wanted to have with the oldest four. Raising five children in Quaint Town, where everyone is under a microscope, was not easy but we weathered that, too. We had our parental challenges just as any parent does and learned quickly how to be a team.

Today, I jokingly say, "we downsized so our children won't come home." Truthfully, I do want them to come home, I just don't want them to stay home. I no longer define myself as a mother of five. I'm my own me. They are their own they.

I, too, have had to let go of what was once "mine," again and again and again and again (at least one is still home!). Yes, they have broken my heart as I broke my Mom's, but it isn't personal, it's parental. When you realize this, your children can become who they are meant to become without your constant supervision. By the time they leave the nest, they should have experienced enough mistakes, falls, accidents, and other problems to navigate this world on their own, holding space for them with love as their safety net. This does not mean you will not get that phone call, yes, our Influenced Self still wants to be needed, however, with the awareness of Influenced Self and our release of attachment, we can still let them fly with the skill set they need to fly, no matter how far they choose to go.

Everyone in your life is an independent soul with unique human experiences. This includes our children.

Our attachments to our relationships and our labels both societal and self-imposed are the figurative chains of suffering. Children, friends, family, work, lovers, all of it can be gone in a moment. These attachments are of the Influenced Self and they are one of the most powerful forces we are challenged with on a moment-by-moment basis.

While the attachments to our children may be the most challenging to deal with, the loss of our parents is a rite of passage and a prime attachment example. Ready or not, your parents will die. It's never easy whether it is sudden or drawn out, you loved them or not. My father passed away right before COVID-19 hit the globe.

"Don't sell Microsoft!," he said.

"OK, Daddy, but do you understand what is going on?" I said, "This virus is crushing the market and Microsoft is taking a big hit."

"Jule," he said, "It will come back. Be patient."

That was my last phone call with him. It was typical of our conversations, short and mostly sweet, despite his ants in the pants to get off the phone. He was telling me to chill out, this too shall pass.

This virus. The stock market. The good. The bad. Life. This moment. A lack of toilet paper. My relationship with my father. Whatever it is, all of it, is fleeting and impermanent. The gift of impermanence isn't this too shall pass. A gift implies a silver lining, a treat, a positive outcome. This too shall pass is the heart wrenching mantra reminding us even the good times pass and to be careful not to wish away everything, good or bad.

The last time I saw my Dad was a month before his passing. It was my sister's birthday and knowing it was her last birthday with him, she and I flew out to be with him,. We walked in on that day, my last day with him and he sang to her, like he sang to everyone on their birthday, a tradition we now try to uphold, even though we barely can get through 'birthday' without breaking down and crying. I remember the last evening with him very well as I sat and just took it all in; his labored breathing, the sounds of MSNBC blaring, the peaceful way he looked as he rested, the uneaten food on his tray, his gnarly feet I massaged for him. I knew this moment was fleeting, as they all are and I decided to just be present with it, with him. I knew I would not see him this way, ever again. So, I took it all in, the laughter, sorrow, love, knowing this too shall pass. With its permanence, death is the harshest lesson in impermanence. Haruki Murakami said, "Pain is inevitable, suffering is optional." No life event challenges this saying more than the death of someone you love.

During the beginning of the pandemic, I listened to people cancel their vacations, wonder about childcare, worry about their adult children, close their small businesses, complain about the out-of-staters buying all the toilet paper in our Quaint Town stores (yes, this happened), and tried not to judge. I tried to simply observe it unfolding. It was not easy, but this spiritual-practice-thing isn't usually easy. When a parent dies, it feels surreal. This happened when my Mom died, too. I wondered why the world did not stop since *my world seemingly did. How could anything be more important than **everyone** stopping what they were doing and acknowledging she was gone? This time though, with everyone reeling from the effects of COVID-19, the sur-reality of our realities, was palpable, just not for the same reasons.*

The family's attachment to my father, his attachment to us (and Microsoft) made it challenging for him to ultimately let go. There was a way I wanted to say goodbye. I wanted to be there when he died but I lived across the country and as COVID started ramping up, so did restrictions on traveling to and from our state. For a long time, I held on to how I wanted to be there for him, how I thought I could help him pass easier (you know, I'm so enlightened and all that). My attachment to how I wanted things to go, was the cause of great suffering. This too shall pass. He did and ultimately so has my suffering.

Presence is the gift of impermanence. It allows you to transcend attachment into letting go. Sit back, look around, take it in. The good and the bad. Yes, people will disappoint you, but they will also impress you. Just like the last night in that hospital room with my Dad; there was the good (his peaceful rest) and the bad (those feet!), both equally important.

This too shall pass but do not let it pass without noticing and certainly try to approach it with peace instead of clinging or attachment. It is going to be ok. The lucky ones are those who recognize the gift of impermanence. Those who do will be moved by deeply human experiences, have far less anxiety and their lives will be richer for it. I know mine is. I will never forget that night. I never even want to forget those feet.

Attachment and the way we choose to handle changes to our attachments is an integral part to recognizing the Other – everyone has attachments, and they can cause great suffering. Embracing these changes in your own life helps you empathize with the Other's attachment plight.

The attachment examples I gave above are pretty heavy duty – children and parents. I didn't even touch on spouses or partners! Those relationships may not be the best place to start your "everything is borrowed" practice but you do want to integrate some sort of letting go into your daily life. Consider other attachments – your favorite coffee shop changes their menu, the closing of a favorite restaurant, a job change, a health challenge, an expected or unexpected transition, a move, etc. Try not to react. Make peace with the change in circumstance by releasing the grip of attachment. Feel these moments. This is life. Being in the moment, appreciating the impermanence of everything in our lives. When we realize the gift of impermanence, the deep awareness of the present moment and embrace its fleetingness, our lives become fuller even if experiencing this fullness comes from loss. I can guarantee you, life will throw you many opportunities to practice letting go.

Letting Go
Practice and Prompts

You can take baby steps with practicing letting go. Add it to your practice.

S   M   T   W   Th   F   S

Influenced
Self
- stressor
- breathe
- release
- truth
Letting Go

Try giving away something that isn't super special to you. Now give away something you love.

What about giving up a favorite food or routine you love? What does this feel like?

What does that moment feel like just before you donate a beloved belonging, or you have eaten a favorite treat for the last time?

What do those moments feel like when you are with whatever you may be choosing to release?

What if we were always aware that it could be our "last" time, moment or situation? How would that change how we show up?

Are you clinging to certain people in your life? Do you think your children (or your pets) belong to you?

Judgment becomes Acceptance

When we are in a state of acceptance, we love our friends instead of being critical and we are willing to love them despite their limitations, which we willingly overlook. The way people appear to us from this space is that everyone is actually doing the best they can with what they have now at the moment.

David Hawkins, *Letting Go*

If I had made my mantra, "Everyone is doing the best they can with what they have at the moment," my life would have been filled with far less drama.

My marriage would have still ended but under more honorable circumstances (Influenced Self!) and with a lot less pain (The Other) had I not been so judge-y. My judging led to my justifying, justifying a move away from Suit and ultimately an affair. Blaming him for his compulsive ways, resenting him for our money problems over the years, and his obsession with work, took the onus off my role. These stories I told myself about our relationship aren't true. I now know, relationships are 50/50. We don't always show up daily with 100% of our 50% part, but that is a marriage. And when one ends, you have to own your role. I do now. It took a long time and truth be told, there are times when I feel myself being pulled into old patterns. It is in those times when I must remember to continue to practice my newfound habits. Trying as it might be.

Habitual judging isn't conducive to making any relationship work. It pulls people apart. Start practicing with strangers – in traffic, at Starbucks, in the grocery store. Our work is to change judgment into acceptance and learn to observe without our biased thoughts attached.

Here is an everyday example you can learn from immediately (which would be way faster than me).

Checking out at the grocery store recently, the cashier was acting rudely towards me. She was annoyed the produce I had chosen was not marked and the chicken I had purchased was making a mess at her station. The line of customers was backing up, I was running late, heat flushing my face as she calls for help on a price check. Huffing and puffing, she pulls out paper towels to clean the mess, muttering under her breath and not making eye contact with me.

I was beginning to feel upset, the first sign my Influenced Self is getting involved. And although, I am aware of this, it didn't keep me from getting a bit heated. After all, it isn't my fault the chicken was leaking, and the produce isn't labeled. (Influenced Self Values: Accountability, Determination, Power)

I have three options here:

a.) respond with my own rude remark,

b.) report her to the manager,

or c.) acknowledge that she too has a life full of pressures and circumstances I know nothing about, chalking it up to having to be the recipient of her human experience.

If I had changed the story, one acknowledging she has her stuff and so do I, this situation would not need to escalate to become the clash of the Influenced Selves. If I simply thanked her and wished her a good day, how would that have felt? (Brownie points: I try to give her a quiet blessing as I walk out the door). Situation diffused. This had nothing to do with who I really am or who she really is for that matter, but everything to do with two Influenced Selves potentially colliding, each trying desperately to defend itself. By changing my story to facts, not fiction I avoided the drama.

As soulful humans, ones who are working on finding our souls, we need to express ourselves in ways that do not take down others. In the grocery store, had I responded rudely with Option A to that cashier the situation would have escalated. I told myself a story about why she was being rude to me, she was attacking me for choosing unlabeled produce and messy chicken. My Influenced Self needed protection.

Option B, reporting her to the manager is still coming from the Ego because again, it is based on a story in my mind. Is it a fact that she was rude? Maybe. Let's say I chose (b) and went to the manager. "Excuse me, the cashier on checkout lane 5 was rude to me." Even if I just stopped there, can you see the Influenced Self? Who cares that she was rude to me? There were facts - there was no label on the produce and the chicken was leaking. Her reaction to it is her stuff, not mine. Those are her stories in her mind, not my concern. I should only be concerned with bringing awareness to my stories and putting a halt on what I can control - my overreaction (and maybe next time choosing labeled produce and squared away chicken!).

Option C would have been a sweet choice. I didn't choose "c," I chose "b" (I told you this spiritual thing takes a long time as this wasn't that long ago). I felt a little high and mighty, or dare I say entitled and then every time I saw her thereafter, I felt badly because I did not consider her story. Had I avoided the drama in the first place, the drama would no longer linger. Don't worry, not that you were, but I'm getting better at this non- judgment thing. I get plenty of daily practice.

In *A New Earth* by Eckhart Tolle, he shares a beautiful example of two ducks on a pond having a conflict but because they are ducks, they don't judge (nor do they attach any other emotions to the conflict). Duck A gets too close to Duck B's pond space. Duck B flaps his wings, does some squawking, and shoos the other duck away. Duck B's squawking and wing flapping was his way to release the emotion he felt being intruded upon, just like our grocery clerk. Duck A may have been innocently in Duck B's space, who knows, but either way, they go their separate ways after the encounter without any grudges. I am not saying you need to flap your wings and let out the steam, I am saying, when you walk away, you do not need to hold on to the emotions you may have wanted to act on. Let it go!

The human experience gives us LOTS of practice in Influenced-Self-identification. Converting our *judgments* into *acceptance* allows us to move through this spiritual phase and transcend to a place where our True Self has room to show up when that moment of grace appears. Where we recognize we are all doing the best we can with what we have. It isn't personal. Our Influenced Self makes it personal.

Dealing with cashiers at grocery stores is one thing. Things get dicey when they hit closer to home. Here is one such scenario.

Stay-at-home-sick Guy (formerly Gym-Crush) was unable to work at the gym we own together. So, I am running the show at the gym. We both have training clients, teach classes and additionally

he wears the maintenance hat while I wear the hat the covers everything else. So, I am wearing his hat, and mine, teaching my classes, covering his classes, holding down the house fort, making sure he had what he needed, picking up, dropping off and taking care of Youngest and all of his needs. Additionally, Oldest Son was home for a college break.

Let's say we were now on Day 3. This particular day, I had been up since 5:30 am, taught, trained, ran to the store for Stay-at-home-sick Guy, picked up, dropped off said youngest, cooked dinner in the middle of the day, went back to work and came home around 7 pm. I walked in the door to "What's for dinner?" from Youngest. To which I regroup, cook some rice (forgot to do this midday) and slopped chicken, rice and a salad onto four plates. At which point, I realize the dishwasher hadn't been emptied and the laundry was backing up. I scarf down my food, empty the dishwasher (super pissed at Oldest Son) and run some laundry. Is Stay-at-home sick Guy so sick he cannot do laundry?

I run upstairs to ask Stay-at-home sick Guy "Will you be working tomorrow?"

To which he replies, "No way."

I grab my phone, begin to adjust my next day (canceling and moving clients) so I can teach his classes. He then says, "You are ALWAYS on your phone!" Really? Please tell me he is kidding.

I am pretty pissed right now. Does he even have a clue what I've been doing for the past three days? Does he have any idea how I busted my butt today for him and the boys? Are the boys helpless? How have I failed them, or worse have I failed their future wives? I am apologizing in my head, to their future wives. More stories. I decide to shower without a reply. Telling even more stories in my *mind, recounting everything in my head, over and over.*

This was all about my myths, the stories I was running in my head, about the boys and Stay-at-home sick Guy. He felt crappy. He had been missing me. The boys were hungry. When boys are hungry, it is not pretty. They are too primal to think about anything else besides being fed - it actually may be impossible for them but again, this a story I have made up (but is probably true). I was overworked, tired and felt unappreciated (another story). So, I went upstairs after my shower and kissed Stay-at-home-sick Guy goodnight and did not talk about my emotions for a few days. The timing wasn't right.

When emotions are flaring you have to change the story, change the voice inside your head. No not David Byrne's mantra "How did I get here?", but your story, the story you are telling yourself. In this case, 'He doesn't have a clue what I do for him daily' needed some editing. By walking away, I gave myself (and him) some space and purposefully changed my thoughts. This was my Influenced Self getting in the way. All the attacks I thought were on me were not about me. I was taking it personally, but it wasn't personal. He was telling himself stories; the boys were focused on the story their stomachs were telling them and I was focused on the pity party they were not throwing me. It does not matter who is right or wrong, it just is and most of it is not true, just roles with attached stories.

In the case of loved ones, you do have to live with them and love them. You cannot just walk out of the house never expecting to resolve whatever just went down, like at the grocery store with the cashier. There is no manager to rat them out to. You will want to resolve these situations, but at a different time, without emotion, without stories; 'You were wrong, and I was right.' These little storms and stories with resolution enforce the bond and encourage growth together. You show up as the adult you want to be, the one you agreed to be when you entered into the relationship in the first place. Not everyone acts like the adult so just make peace with this reality. You don't need to explain to the people in your life that their Influenced Self is getting in the way. That isn't your job, as tempting as it might be. It also may cause other problems with other stories.

A note on the difference between enabling (in the relationship sense) and non-reactive observation. Enabling is supporting someone's self-destructive behavior. Observation is allowing yourself the space to be non-reactive in a situation's heat and acknowledging the different perspectives at a better time. Observation is productive and healthy because it takes into consideration both sides. Enabling is neither as it is primarily concerned with supporting one person's negative behavior without resolution. Observation brings the relationship closer. Enabling builds walls. As the Observer, you can bring attention to this toxic relationship trait. Remaining in your Influenced Self without observation does not recognize the enabler. Take it from a pro.

The next time you find yourself getting emotional, you must think about the other person's perspective, the story they may be telling themselves and the myth that may be at play here – in this case, judgment. Remove yourself from the situation if possible and regroup. Our relationships make this more challenging, but when we can work on that, we will find more acceptance.

For me, a simple exchange from an acquaintance was one of the biggest awakenings in my life. A woman who was a member at our gym, wrote me a short email. Clearly upset, she wrote, "you don't ever give me the time of day. It's as if you are in your own world." Another sign? Probably. At first glance, I was upset with her for calling me out on my behavior. I felt attacked and took it personally. I have five kids. I'm running a business. I'm working 30 plus hours – of course, I am in my own world, what other world could I possibly be in?

But then I took a moment and thought about this one, well maybe not just for a moment, for a long time, actually. This simple email from a disgruntled member. As a business owner, I hadn't given much thought to the fact that people have different needs, beyond the desire for a cool place to exercise. I was pretty self-absorbed. I justified it with the knowledge that we provided a great place to work out, we worked hard training clients, and keeping the gym clean, but I never really considered individual personal needs. She needed me to acknowledge her and make small talk. This was something as an Introvert I didn't do well and needed to work on, not just for her, but also for myself which ultimately benefits all day-to-day interactions. This fact taught me to question two things: Who am I to others? and Who are others to me? It was then that I really realized we are playing roles in this life and when we are stuck in these roles, we take things very personally. And it's not personal. It never is. It is perspective.

Here is where the three sides and the truth come to fruition. I am a mother and gym owner. I've got all kinds of stories attached to both of those labels. She was a customer and had certain expectations I needed to meet while she was playing that role. My stories did not jive with her stories, and somewhere in the middle was the truth. I did not understand her perspective and she did not understand mine, we each had our sides of the same story. She was taking my aloofness personally, and I took her email as an attack. Neither are true. The truth is we both have heavy overlay (Influenced Selves colliding) and by recognizing this and the fact we are both soulful beings, brings levity to the conflict and depth to the encounter, providing growth to both of us. We are actually very friendly now, with a deeper understanding of one another.

Acknowledging there is a truth somewhere in between, is enough. Proving we know this truth is not our job.

We can learn from these signs and the feelings they trigger whether it is an email, chance encounter, miracle, or deep relationship. These are the signs our Influenced Self covers up with stories. In the book, *The Four Agreements* by Don Miguel Ruiz, the second agreement is "Don't Take Anything Personally." This concept took me a very long time to completely understand. In a nutshell, I have my stuff and you have your stuff and neither one has much to do with the other, so don't take whatever comes up as an attack. It has nothing to do with you. Ruiz doesn't quite say it like that, but that is what he means, and it is a much healthier way to live. Shower the situation with acceptance and I can guarantee, you will find more spiritual growth and a peaceful heart.

Most of us spend our days judging ourselves or others. This is THE BIGGEST SPIRITUAL CHALLENGE you will face. You will need a lot of practice to stop judging, and you will get a lot of practice: on the phone, in person, with your sibling, parent, spouse, partner, friend, co-worker, employee, boss, stranger, wherever, whenever. It is everywhere, and it is up to us to recognize and fill the space with acceptance.

You will know that judgment is creeping in when you vocalize your biased opinion. This isn't truth. You think this is truth. It's a myth. Catch yourself in the story. Catch others in the story (without telling them you caught them because that too is judgment). Close your mouth and let acceptance permeate the space you are holding at the moment. Remember everyone has their perspective. You don't need to agree with it at the moment, just accept it. There is no right or wrong, it just is. With acceptance, Soul shows up in the form of love and all feels more right with the world. Take a breath and sit with that now. The Universe gives you plenty of opportunities to practice. Plenty.

The beliefs we have about others, are just that, fabricated in our minds. It isn't until we can recognize the Other as part of our humanity, as part of We, not Us vs Them, that our spiritual journey unfolds – we are all connected. Yes, this might mean not judging your friend when she talks about all the hardships going on in her life, or not fighting the fight with your Conservative sibling when you are a Liberal, or any other judgment we hold on to as truth, which it isn't. Changing judgment to acceptance is the path to liberation and to uncovering our lost souls.

Acceptance
Practice and Prompts

Begin to bring awareness to your
judgments throughout your day.
Turn your judgments into acceptance.

Influenced Self   S   M   T   W   T   F   S
- stressor
- breathe
- release
- truth

Setting Go

Acceptance

What situation did I encounter today where I caught myself ready to judge but chose not to?

What was the emotional trigger?

What did it feel like not to judge?

Did a disagreement become emotional and in turn, judgmental?

Reflect on how a disagreement could have been handled differently.

How does acceptance feel?

Control becomes Surrender

I don't mind what happens.

J. Krishnamurti

There is a story about the philosopher Krishnamurti where he promises to give a lecture revealing his secret to life. He gets on stage and states those five words, "I don't mind what happens" and walks off. His followers were shocked that his life work boiled down to five words. What is more shocking, is the simple truth in those words.

We have no control, absolutely none. The sooner we can recognize this, embrace the "I don't mind what happens" philosophy, the more freedom we have from its grip. It's this lack of control, and the struggle to gain control, that causes most of our suffering. No one has control over external circumstances, ever. When you recognize your role in these situations you can quickly discern what you can control: your reaction. No one else. No-thing else.

During the time of this writing, Covid-19 is a global pandemic. In the United States more than 800,000 people have died and this number grows daily. What is the big COVID-19 lesson? I ponder this question often. In my opinion, the greatest lesson of COVID-19 is we do not have control. Yes, we can control our behavior, but not anyone else's. Yes, we can control what we do in the situation, but we cannot control the situation. In our case, when COVID struck and lockdown was implemented, our gym closed. We had to pivot. We did. In other cases, far more complicated and life altering, the

head of the household loses a job, and the family is financially devastated. A family member gets sick, and we can't see them. Or worse, we cannot be there for the death of a loved one. Heartbreaking.

So many experiences during this COVID crisis and most come down to wanting to control the outcome and being unable to do so. You feel helpless. Everyone does. It feels like we cannot get our footing. Depression, suicide, domestic abuse, all on the rise, all because of this desperation and helplessness, the lack of control and the fight within us to hold on to what was. A fruitless fight. Let go of the illusion of control. That is exactly what it is, an illusion.

When the world feels crazy, we must step back. Ask ourselves, what are we missing here? What is the bigger picture? What can I learn from even the most seemingly devastating of circumstances? This gives perspective and this perspective leads to surrender. This is true about every situation that feels out of control. Step back, let it unfold, stop forcing the situation. Trying to control other people and situations comes from the Influenced Self and it always backfires. It creates stress and if you are truly looking for your Essence, your True Self, the life force within, your Soul, stress is not only uninvited, but there also isn't any space at the table for it. Only you can make this choice. And yes, you do have control over your choices.

With this step back, this observation, we turn control into surrender. If our behavior is only about surrendering, and the rest we leave to the Universe, then the Universe gets the message that we are confident and comfortable with the unknown, and things begin to fall into place.

When we can surrender, allowing an unfolding to take place, the Universe answers the call, turning the finite possibilities into the infinite. This is faith.
This is surrendering to the mystery.

The Universe realizes you are no longer fighting what is. Surrender. Go back to your breath. Become the Observer. Maybe even notice the lesson or signs. We do not have control. Surrender to that truth and do what you can – control your response.

Surrender
Practice and Prompts

Let's add surrender to your practice.

Influenced Self   S   M   T   W   T   F   S
- stressor
- breathe
- release
- truth

Setting Go

Acceptance

Surrender

What are you trying to control?

Who are you trying to control?

If a disagreement spoiled the moment,
     ask yourself:

    Is this personal?

    Is my Influenced Self playing a role

   What is the other person's perspective?

   What are the facts?

   Is this true?

   What am I holding on to?

The Awakened Values

When you have awakened to the Observer and notice the world around you, you begin to live in a more community-minded value system. Below is a list of these values.

Advocacy   Balance   Community
Compassion   Connection   Contribution
Cooperation   Diversity   Empathy
Encouragement   Enthusiasm   Fairness
Generosity   Honesty   Humility
Integrity   Kindness   Openness
Optimism   Patience   Peace
Respect (when given)   Responsibility
Service   Stewardship   Teamwork
Thoughtfulness   Trust   Understanding
Vision   Warmth

These values remind us of the Other,
what we say and do matters.

Play with integrating them into
your spiritual practice.

How do they feel?

How do letting go, acceptance and
surrender play out in these values?

Space

Space – The final frontier.

Captain Kirk, *Star Trek*

Captain Kirk was on to something. Space is our final frontier, especially when it comes to the Other. Giving people space means rising above yourself as a form, rising to higher consciousness. Learning to let go, accept and surrender makes room in our relationships, it gives us space. Notice this space, this breath, your non reaction, and witness your True Self. Our lost souls are found.

What does this mean? It means when a conflict arises, take a moment. Sit with the conflict. Truly listen. When you want to interject, advise, or just butt in, don't. Attachment, Judgment, Control are all falsehoods, drama feeding the Influenced Self. Acknowledge the fact that you are clinging to attachment then let it go. Acknowledge the judgments (stories) that are popping in your head and soften them with acceptance. Recognize when you are trying to control a situation and surrender.

When we give space to others, we experience our True Selves, our Essence, our Soul, and the coolest part of getting a glimpse of this is we recognize The Other as a soul. When we realize The Other is also a soul, and not just as an independent Influenced Self human, it is much easier to turn attachment into letting go, judgment into acceptance and control into surrender. When all we can control is our behavior, our reaction, we can choose to make sacrifices, be it in work or personal life because of a greater good. We are all soulful beings, and what we do matters, what we do affects us all. *There is no Other.* Give yourself some space right now to let that concept seep in. *There is no Other.*

Looking back on all of my Influenced Self stories, this concept is so clear, but nothing gave me more insight into this concept than my experience in a local prison.

It was cold, well at least I was cold or just incredibly nervous. That's what nerves do to me, give me the shivers. I was just reprimanded for wearing a hoodie, so I took it off and stashed it into a worn-out locker, the only thing not secure in here. The guard waited with me while Control Center controlled the Center, granting us permission to enter when it was safe enough.

The cement block walls were painted light green, not a pretty light green but not horrid either. BUZZZZZZZZ. The door latch unlocks, the guard opens it for me, we enter. SLAM, the door startles me as it bangs behind us, jolting my already nervous energy. By the third time, I was getting a little more used to it. I guess that is what happens when I hear it enough, I get used to it in here. I am sure there are many things I will get used to here. We are finally at my destination. How did I get here?

I walk into the office, the nameplate on a desk reads "Director of Recreation." The office was lined with that light green cinderblock, crowded with two metal desks, one for her, my supervisor, the other for her supervisor. Behind her desk were the "reward" shelves, the baskets filled with treats the women would receive if they showed up to her fitness classes, including Skittles, candy bars, shampoo, soaps and playing cards. Delight was the name of my supervisor at the women's correctional facility where I had been volunteering for a couple of months now. We were to discuss a Health and Wellness Program I planned to implement.

"I'd like to be a part of this," she said.

I said, "Sure, what are you thinking?"

She continued, "I think they need to write an essay about why they don't like to exercise to get into the program."

Hmm, write an essay about why they do not like to exercise? Between this idea and the fact, she was rewarding exercise with Skittles and candy bars, I knew already we were not on the same page.

Confused by this idea, I said, "I'm not sure that is the best motivator. I have been in physical fitness for over 17 years, and I have never seen anyone motivated to exercise by writing an essay about why they do not want to exercise. I'm just not sure this makes sense."

Frustrated with my response, she said "Well, you don't have the experience I have, and this will work. I know how to motivate them. I have been doing this a long time, too. You clearly don't know how motivation works or have the same experience I do."

True enough, she has got me there. I have never worked in a Correctional Facility, but I have worked with women, many in fact and never would a woman, or for that matter anyone, be motivated to exercise by writing an essay about why they hate it.

I explained to her, "I'm not going to be part of a program where this is a punishment. It isn't motivating, it does not make sense to me and no one will want to write an essay to earn gym time. That certainly will not be my approach to this program. I have never heard of punishing people to motivate them to exercise. The military punishes people through exercise, but we aren't in the military here and it doesn't motivate them to exercise if they are forced to do that."

I had already gotten approval for the program and didn't need hers. I certainly wasn't going to rely on her so-called help. I'm not a confrontational person, but when she questioned my skillset and suggested we essentially punish the women before they even started, I had to push back. I had seen her power-trip, but I hadn't been the recipient of it, until this moment. Strange she thought she could speak to me this way.

During the weeks leading up to this, I had witnessed many instances of her superiority trip. The first time was when I saw her walking around the gym with her hands in the letter "T", not saying a word. She was apparently letting the women know it was time to end their workout but with zero communication, just walking up to them, showing her two hands forming a "T" in their faces. This made me feel very uneasy and the inmates looked at me and rolled their eyes. 'Delight'? Anything but that. She treated them like preschoolers. Why can't she just announce an ending to the session? "Ladies, gym time is over. Finish up your routine". Sounds easy enough.

Admittedly, when I was first introduced to the inmates, I sat in judgment about their facial tattoos, attitudes, and what got them into this mess. I was intimidated actually. Though I felt intimidated, I also felt superior. I remember twisting my wedding ring nervously, realizing I had forgotten to leave it at home, wondering what might happen if they noticed it, fielding their questions about my motives. Feeling uncomfortable, I had begun to question my motives, too. Why would a woman from Quaint Town volunteer here? Of course, *there is the I-want-to-make-a-difference-motive. My co-worker and friends back home thought I was crazy. But something about the prison pulled me to it. I can't fully explain why.*

Carl Jung said, "Everything that irritates us about others can lead us to an understanding of ourselves."

Finding truth in this quote takes a solid dose of humility and Delight was seriously irritating me. What was her behavior trying to show me about myself? I am superior? Me vs. Them?

I wondered if Delight was reflecting my ego, the reason for thinking class categories exist, the belief in the falsehood there are inferior and superior people. Truth be told, I have felt superior walking through a Walmart or watching rural Americans on TV voice their love for a seemingly unfit political candidate. On the flip side, I have felt inferior at a fancy hotel, restaurant or spa where I simply wanted to run for the door, feeling completely uncomfortable, out of place. Do other people feel better than or less than? Do other people feel both? What makes us feel this way? Ego?

When I compartmentalize people – Supervisor, Volunteer, Inmate, am I dehumanizing them? Can I shed labels and simply observe others as human, no one higher, no one lower? Do I have to relinquish my Ego in order to see this Truth? Is this even possible?

Ultimately, it really didn't matter where I came from, or where they came from, what society labeled us, or the stories we have attached to those labels, or even why or how any of us got there. Witnessing Delight's superiority while forging my own sisterhood with the inmates, helped me grow and learn, exposing a falsehood to which I clung, another story.

Superior . Inferior .

I knew I was called to this facility, besides the fact, six months ago, Astrologer told me I would be working with women. With my ego exposed, I think I may have been called to experience a universal Truth:

When I acknowledge we are equally human, there is no longer the Other, and we become one in our sameness.
If there is no Other then We are One.

Another story? No, this is a fact. The Truth of One.

Let me tell you, this just didn't happen when I showed up at the Facility, meeting Delight with her superiority-trip. This took years. Years and years. But you can't search, question, or wonder while you are figuratively sleeping through life, like so many of us are, like I was, which is why this took me so long. Raising children, having loved and lost, being a contributing member to my community, recognizing The Other, having deep spiritual experiences, all of this leads to that one big Truth.

We are One.

When you go through life with this realization, a seismic shift in consciousness happens. You look into the eyes of another human, a total stranger, someone who doesn't look or act like you, maybe even from a totally different background and you see them, just like the Na'vi in *Avatar* do. You see your soul reflected from theirs. "I see You."

Our search for our souls just got a whole lot easier. It has nothing to do with circumstances outside of us and everything to do with acknowledging the other as part of the whole.

This happens when you see people, not for the roles and

stories you have fabricated but for who they really are, divine just like you. That space between words, breaths, moments, is divine intervention and we can capture it at any time. It feels like synchronicity, that all is ok in the world. It is a feeling of peace, of love. A field of infinite possibilities has room to show up because with love, anything is possible.

After you awaken from your Influenced Self and we grow from thinking there is The Other to We are One, the next phase is Live with Intention. It is time to give *yourself* space. Living fully, by being present to the moment is the one thing we can count on in this world and is the portal to discovering your True Self, your true gifts and how we can show up in the world, fully present, and awake. By coming home to ourselves, our Souls, we shine our light. Just like Lizzo says, "If I'm shining, everybody's gonna shine."

Live with Intention

The Argument for Meditation

This is our work, to discover what we can give.

Robin Wall Kimmerer, *Braiding Sweetgrass*

You may not want to hear this, but meditation is the vessel to understanding present moment awareness, the portal to your True Self, your Soul. The miracle of meditation is the space it gives you, and the awareness it brings to give space to others. Meditation is a very personal experience. I believe there is no one right way. There are many books, apps and advice on this subject. Explore them. What resonates with you? Try different modalities. This will become your next practice.

It took me a very long time to give myself permission to meditate the way I wanted to meditate. No cushions, chanting, mantras, or guided meditations ended up being the right fit. It was not without an abundance of trial and error. For a year, I meditated every morning for an hour, yes, an hour. It was a priority for me. I woke up early and did it. But then it no longer suited me. Now, for me, truthfully, I lie in bed and meditate for 8-10 minutes before I get out of bed and before I go to sleep. I focus on my breath, observing my physical self, releasing thoughts that are vying for my attention, clearing my head with a deep presence and blank slate. It wasn't without trying many versions of meditation that I found my own way. I've given myself permission to find what works for me because just like exercise, something is way better than nothing and eventually you too will find what works for you.

Meditation opens the space between breaths, between thoughts and that is consciousness, the no-thingness of no-thought. Your presence for this space, where there are no stories, attachments, judgments, control, or any other ego intrusion is the same space of your True Self, your Higher Self, your Essence, your Soul. When this space is held for you personally or for others in your life, love enters. This love is unconditional, pure and innocent. Just like the light that tugged on my blankets that night all those years ago. Love shows up when our soulful practices are honored. Our souls are quite simply pure love.

Meditation feels like another dimension, one without the constraints of humanness, it's where our being-ness happens. Some call this God, others might say the Universe, Him, Her, They. It doesn't matter what you call it. You will notice you are one with it and the drama and stresses of our human experience fade away. The tricky thing about meditation is it's so beautiful and peaceful, you may not want to leave it and return to our ordinary human being-ness. But we can take it with us in the form of giving space. Space for yourself. Space for the ones you love. Space for total strangers.

This is what happens with presence. Things slow down. You can sense the space, the peace, the love, the synchronicity of it. This is the definition of Heaven. Heaven is not up in the clouds somewhere, or in our next lives. Heaven is right here.

Meditation allows you the space to discover your present moment awareness. Meditation is the portal to Heaven.

When you can tap into this presence, this inner purpose of just being one with the moment, it is as if everything is flowing. There is no swimming upstream. It allows you to show up for you. It allows you to show up for others. When you are living on purpose you are fully and completely in the moment. Complete awareness to the moment. It is all we truly have. If we spend our lives feeling guilty about the past, or worrying about the future, there is no presence. You are missing out on what truly matters. This moment and only this moment. Right here. Right now.

When you can show up for yourself, and for others, your true light shines. This is the beginning of living with intention, feeling on purpose. This space, this presence, roots you in the moment and the hang-ups of your Influenced Self fade away.

I first really noticed this idea of flow, presence, living on purpose, when I was meeting with my book club one evening.

I am not great in groups, but apparently the Universe does not care, when her whispers challenged me to start a Spiritual Book Club. I listened begrudgingly and put it out there. I got 14 responses which is kind of a lot for Quaint Town. This Introvert would now have to put her big girl pants on and socialize. Little did I know how life-changing this experience would be.

Our meeting was coming up and we had been reading The Prophet by Kahlil Gibran. Saying 'I struggled with this book' is an understatement That is the beauty/problem with a book club, with commitment comes commitment. And since I'm a rule follower, it follows I forced myself to read it.

The poetry and artistry of this bestseller was beyond me. I am ridiculously literal so the metaphors throughout this book were well let us say, a struggle. I simply did not get it. I plugged along through the book trying to find some meaning.

Where are the how-to lists?

Where are the definitive answers to my incessant meaning-of-life questions?

Why does this book sound like the Bible?

Kahlil, throw me a bone! I felt clueless. How would I possibly lead this group? I'm not capable.

So, I did what every poetry-averse, group leading Introvert would do: I Googled a cheat sheet and took notes on it. There you go, you've got this.

The women arrived and we settled in. I fessed up immediately. This former Catholic Girl has zero poker-face. I wasn't about to bumble my way through this one or pretend I understood why millions of other readers loved this book. All the preparation in the world was not going to help me. Google proved not to be my 'phone a friend.' I was dreading this.

Then something unexpected happened. The women in the group picked out favorite passages and interpreted them for me. They shared without reservation. We were laser-like present, inquisitive, and non-judgmental. We gave each other space and because of this space, we grew closer. We wanted to hear each other and learn. We challenged one another but not in a competitive way, in a supportive way. We laughed. We cried. We reflected. We were what Brené Brown refers to, in her multi-million times viewed Ted Talk, as vulnerable. This vulnerability brought us closer. Suddenly, Mr. Gibran's work was making sense and I could see the beauty. She CAN be taught!

This experience is what Priya Parker refers to in her book, The Art of the Gathering. In it, she goes into great detail about a Japanese saying Ichi go, Ichi e, (pronounced Itchy go Itchy A). It means "one opportunity, one encounter" or "for this moment only." Set as an intention, it brings a deep sense of sacredness to the present. Every moment is fleeting. Every moment will never happen again. Life is fleeting. Revel in it. Ichi go, Ichi e. That day in my book club, we did not set this intention, but it felt like we did. Presence made this meeting special and uniquely beautiful. We walked out knowing we were somehow changed by this experience.

Now, imagine taking this concept to your next meeting, book club, chance encounter or passionate love-making session; giving this kind of space, support and curiosity, this kind of deep presence, filled with reverence and beauty. It's the difference between making a moment memorable or not. All of these moments will feel more connected, fulfilling, and uniting.

I'm so thankful those Universal whispers were loud enough for me to hear. I learned the power of vulnerability, the power of this moment, the power of the collective, the power of space, all of which is far more powerful than the one.

Presence feels like watching life unfold, and while you may feel sometimes like you are disconnected, it is only the detachment from the Influenced Self. It is not from the person involved or from the feelings for that person. In fact, what actually happens is the complete opposite, a total connection with the present moment, with that person or situation. This is a lifelong practice on your path. Non-attachment with the stories, but deep awareness with the present moment.

With Presence Comes Possibilities

When the basis for your actions is inner alignment with
the present moment, your actions become empowered
by the intelligence of Life itself.

Eckhart Tolle, *A New Earth*

Having practiced meditation and present moment awareness allowed me to experience one of the most spiritual moments of my entire life. A visit from my mother.

While I look forward to visiting family at Thanksgiving time, the past 20 Thanksgivings have had a tinge of sadness, marking the anniversary of my mom's passing. Over the years, I would think of my mom now and again, but never pursued a real connection with her on the other side. I had started and stopped my spiritual work many times but after years of starting and stopping, I decided to stay the course.

Youngest Son and I were away on a soccer weekend together in West Virginia one recent summer, when I was reading the book Signs by Laura Lynne Jackson. The book is filled with stories of people connecting with their loved ones who have passed. I didn't need convincing. I knew this could happen it just never happened to me. The author mentions making a very specific list about the loved one who has passed so that when a connection is made there would be zero doubt. Hmm, let's see. Frank Sinatra. Paul Newman. The Bee Gees song "More Than A Woman" (my mother mistakenly thought it was "Bald headed woman"), cinnamon rolls, crows etc.

I was instructed to set the intention to connect, being very specific about the place and time. OK, here I go. "Mom, will you show up at Youngest Son's game tomorrow?"

The next day at the game, it was about 99 degrees with 99% humidity. Being the good mom that I am, I was entirely focused on the game and the fact that I was melting. So, an encounter with my mom was not on my radar....at all. Truthfully, I had completely forgotten about my intention. I just wanted to be alive by the end of the game. I was watching his game, but I was not on alert for what could be a sign. Afterward, we went back to our room to rest and shower when I suddenly thought, 'Did she show up today?' Was that shirt the woman was wearing with the black birds her way of saying 'I'm here!'? Dang, I missed her.

That evening, the team went out for dinner. The adults were all sitting around the table, and I noticed the same woman was wearing the shirt she had on at the game. I thought it was a bit odd that she showed up with it on since we were all sweating to death, and I assumed everyone would have gone back to the hotel to shower and change. I said to her as I pointed to her shirt, "Do you think those birds are crows?" while thinking, 'Mom, was this your sign'? Just as the woman was about to answer, I felt a wave of energy sweep through me, kind of like what you see in the movies when a spirit moves through someone. It was as if

e—v—e—r—y—t—h—i—n—g

w—-a—-s

s—l—-o—-w—-i—n—g

d—o—w—n.

The woman next to me, dressed all in white, screamed, "OH MY GOD! I CAN'T BELIEVE THIS HAPPENED! I'VE NEVER DONE

THIS!" I turned to look at her and she had spilled tomato sauce all over her white clothes. I burst out laughing, then I started crying and blubbering like a crazy person. This was on my list. My mom always spilled food on her white clothes. She could never ever wear white without something happening to it. Everyone was looking at me, very confused as I tried to explain futilely, the book, my mother, the white clothes, the tomato sauce. The author had said those that have passed often use humor to get our attention. Well, my new friend didn't think it was funny, but I sure did. I knew it was my mother and boy did she get my attention.

I've always believed those who have passed live on in the ones they leave behind, whether it's a personality trait or mannerism. I have also always believed they are here with us, a serendipitous visit from a butterfly (or crow in my case) or the playing of a song at an opportune time. When my youngest daughter sneezes, I always smile because she sounds just like my mom. If a crow lands next to my parked car, I think 'there she is.' But now, I have even more proof. Tomato sauce.

I know firsthand I can call on my mom whenever, wherever and she will let me know she is here for me. I will never forget that moment. I hope for many more of them, but not necessarily in the sweltering heat of a summer in West Virginia! I was present, completely absorbed in that moment. A moment with my mom. I wasn't thinking about tomorrow or yesterday. I showed up fully present and she showed up, too.

With presence, you are in the Observer's seat. You see the signs. You recognize the deep connection we have with one another of this earth and beyond. I could not have connected with my mother so deeply had I not been present. This experience didn't need to be 20 years in the making had I learned this lesson of presence sooner. The gift of the present keeps on giving. I can't look back on all of the time I missed out on this treat, (that would be suffering), but I can be here, now, and let the Universe message me as I practice living life wide awake.

So, what does living in the present moment have to do with living with intention? Everything. As we have learned, all moments are fleeting. We only have the present moment. So, spending your days, wishing your work away, is not living the life you were meant to live. You were born to share your gifts with the world. These gifts are uniquely yours. To live on purpose, to live with intention means you spend your time doing deep work, not doing work because you are good at it and get paid well. Doing what you love comes from conscious living. Awake living. Living from the mantra of We are One. We need to carve out time to pursue the things we love. When we do this, we are living with intention.

I understand we can't all just quit our day jobs and jump into charity work. We don't have to do that to be living with intention. Volunteer for something you are passionate about on a weekend once a month. Create something that has been calling you. Make time for these calls from your Soul, from your Muse. Being vulnerable and slightly out of your comfort zone brings true growth.

In Ryder Carroll's book *The Bullet Journal Method*," he describes three scenarios of people following their passions. Only one is able to follow through completely because she took little steps towards it. He goes on to describe a Japanese term *kaizen* which loosely translated means "good change." He states, "By bringing attention to the little things, we can effect change while we avoid overwhelm." So, start small by bringing attention and intention to the moments that matter and your energy towards the things you really want to pursue.

When you are able to bring this reverence more frequently to your time, you will get into flow. Mihaly Csikszentmihalyi, a world-renowned psychologist, is the father of flow and he describes it as follows:

• *Completely involved in what you are doing – focused and concentrated.*

• *A sense of ecstasy – being outside everyday reality.*

•*Greater inner clarity – knowing what needs to be done and how well we are doing*

• *Knowing that activity is doable – that our skills are adequate to the task.*

• *A sense of serenity – no worries about oneself and a feeling of growing beyond the boundaries of ego.*

• *Timelessness – thoroughly focused on the present, hours seem to pass by in minutes.*

• *Intrinsic motivation – whatever produces flow becomes its own reward.*

He never said *flow* is Heaven, but I believe it is. Going with the flow, going deep into the flow, being one with it, that is Heaven. There is no more drama. You are fully present. Living with intention. Living with purpose. Just peace, just like Heaven. You too can live like this. Ilchi Lee in his book *Living Tao* writes, "Awakening to your being in the here and now everyday allows you to feel eternity in this moment." Heaven. Eternity. Same thing.

What does your Heaven look like? I'm in Heaven when I am:

teaching dance.

practicing watercolor.

coaching my clients.

writing.

with my husband, one on one.

with my children (most of the time).

facilitating our spiritual book club.

volunteering at the correctional facility.

deeply involved in a curiosity.

I try to do these activities as often as possible. I want a Heaven-filled life. Follow your interests. Carve out time and get curious. Give this planet your natural gifts and talents. We need them. You too can experience heaven on earth, every day of your life by following your bliss.

Living with Intention
Practice and Prompts

You've been practicing Influenced Self identification, as well as bringing more letting go, acceptance and surrender into your life. Now it is time to integrate shining your light. What small actions can you begin to do, maybe not daily, but at least weekly, that will bring you more joy, allow you to feel on purpose and present, where you are in "flow"? Add these to your dailies. You will be thrilled you did.

Additionally, what kind of meditation practice can you commit to or just try this week?

Influenced Self   S   M   T   W   T   F   S
- stressor
- breathe
- release
- truth

Setting Go

Acceptance

Surrender

Flow

Meditate

What are your strengths? (A great resource for this is Strengths Finder 2.0 by Tom Rath. Buy this book new to receive the code for the online test.)

How can you incorporate your strengths into doing more of what you love?

What activities allow you to experience "flow"?

Life Purpose Exercise

1. List 8-10 moments when I feel "flow."

   Example: When I am teaching
   _____ and my student has an
   "a-ha" moment.

                    When I am creating
   _____ and I lose track of time

2. Pick your top 5 moments and reflect
   on:
   How do these times feel?
      inspired, motivated, connected, on purpose
   What were you doing?
      creating, teaching, working on_____
   Why specifically was it satisfying?
      I am passionate about_____
   What strengths were you using?
      organized, practical, creative

Were you living within your values?

Collaborating, connecting, contributing, advocating

3. Highlight key phrases and rewrite them.

For example:

I get excited to teach people about my newfound knowledge.

I am passionate about helping people reach their goals

4. Write 2-4 sentences using key words / phrases from above?
Choose a few words that inspire, excite, resonate and represent your core strengths and values.
Who or what will you be engaging with?

What is your ultimate goal?

5. Create your Life Purpose Statement
(don't be scared - it can change!)

Example (mine when I began coaching)

My purpose is to use my energy and passion to teach and inspire women to become their strongest physically, emotionally and spiritually through education in wellness, support of self-reflection and the pursuit of knowing.

True Self Values

When we live life from our True Selves, the grace of the Universe unfolds. By living with intention, with purpose, we come home to ourselves. While the list below may feel individualized, it's our best work as individuals that brings us together. Pick a couple and implement them as soon as possible.

Abundance   Acceptance   Adventure
Authenticity   Courage   Creativity
Curiosity   Faith   Forgiveness
Freedom   Fun   Grace
Gratitude   Growth   Hope
Inspiration   Intuition   Joy
Learning   Motivation   Spirituality
Uniqueness   Vulnerability

Conclusion

Final Thoughts

Be the change you wish to see in the world.
Mahatma Gandhi

We can find our lost souls. You may have already seen glimpses. Stay the course, every single day. Living with an open heart, in the present moment, filled with letting go, acceptance and surrender, opens up the possibilities for those True Self values to manifest in your life, in ways you would never expect. When we change, the people around us change, our lives change and thank goodness, our world changes.

The beginning of this book laid out *Merriam-Webster's* definition of enlightenment – being freed from ignorance and misinformation. I'm hopeful by Awakening to the Observer, embracing We are One and Living with Intention, you too feel freedom. With our newfound spiritual practices, we will undoubtedly bring more enlightened moments to our lives - minute by minute, day by day, month by month, for a lifetime of Heaven on earth.

I am your witness, and you are mine. Together, we can do this. *We* will be the solution to the problems of the world, one found soul at a time.

Must-Reads

Lulu Miller *Why Fish Don't Exist**

Thomas Moore *A Religion of One's Own*

Eckhart Tolle *A New Earth**

Don Miguel Ruiz *Four Agreements*

Jay Shetty *Think Like a Monk*

Khalil Gibran's *The Prophet*

David Hawkins *Letting Go*

Priya Parker *The Art of the Gathering*

Robin Wall Kimmerer *Braiding Sweetgrass*

Laura Lynn Jackson *Signs*

Ryder Carroll *The Bullet Journal Method*

Tom Rath *Strength Finders 2.0*

*life-changing

Connect with Julie

juliefarrayroick.com

Instagram: JulieFarrayRoick

ABOUT THE AUTHOR

Julie Roick is a wife, mother,
Board Certified Coach,
writer, personal trainer and
on a spiritual mission.